# LOSING YOUR JOB

*Without*

# LOSING YOUR MIND

## Strategic Ethical Solutions

**KIMBERLY ANN LUSE, Ed.D**

**Losing Your Job Without Losing Your Mind**
Copyright © 2020 by Kimberly Ann Luse, Ed.D.

I want to thank Qat Wanders and her production team for their work on the cover design and formatting expertise. I have been very grateful for the University of Buffalo's School of Social Work's contribution in the realm of trauma-informed care. They have created *The Institute on Trauma and Trauma-Informed Care (ITTIC)* and have generously shared their research findings with the world. Special thanks goes to Shelli Dronsfield, and my mother, my first and greatest teacher, for their masterful editing skills. Finally, I want to thank my teacher, and friend, Katherine Warner. One of the latest lessons she taught me is quite apropos for this book:

Shine your stars.
Feed your workhorses.
Burn your deadwood.
And the heat from the fire will warm the other two.

I dedicate this work to my husband, Evan. He is always standing by my side, helping me remember the most important lesson, which is my intrinsic value to the universe no matter what.

# CONTENTS

# PREFACE

I just celebrated my 57th birthday. And beginning to realize with each passing year there is so much more to learn, so much more to do, so much more to mess up.

That is right. Life is wonderful, scary, frightening, and can be very messy. If you are lucky, it may lead you into messes you never imagined, only so you can emerge a new version of yourself. A version that is scarred, but also stronger; a bit more cynical, but still with an open heart intact.

I once read that life is a series of losses along the way. Losing your childhood innocence. Losing friends, lovers, and family members. Losing contests. Losing jobs. The ultimate loss at the end of the reading was losing your physical life on earth.

I would like to add my voice and suggest that I am discovering that I am learning to lose negative pieces of life as the years fall away. The regrets that once consumed me are lessening with the real work that I am doing to identify them, and exorcise them, one by one. It is a constant, sometimes annoying journey, but one I have learned is filled with great, great reward. The work must be done internally, of course, but also with the trusted support of others who will work to build you up, not tear you down. At some point, the decision must be made: do I release myself from the external as well as self-inflicted wounds from the past? Or make amends with myself and others and move forward into the new dawn searching for my better self?

The chapters that follow were written with the intent to speak to my readers from the heart. I hope that it will reach anyone who travels through the pages in meaningful ways. As I continue my work as a coach, mentor and trainer, I have seen an all too common false belief that has become hardwired for people. The belief that your job title defines who you are, and ultimately your worth. At one point, I believed this particular false notion myself. It came to a terrible, glaring crossroads the day I was fired from a job. But from those ashes I came to a new truth.

It is simply this: I am me. I am not my job. So many times, we fall down a dark hole when our professional plans go sideways. Without the lapel pin, the company picnic, the holiday party, well, who are we anyway? How do we get to a place so stilted that it feels that absent a title, or position, we are somehow lesser human beings? To a person I say, "You Are You. You Are Not Your Job." Know it is possible to lose your job without losing your mind.

How do we keep that in perspective? And keep the blinders from becoming so dark we do not know the difference? I have a few things to share about what I have learned along the way. Some are from my personal experiences. Most are from the learning I have taken from others as they graciously share their experiences with me. Some are funny, some are joyous, some suck. At the end of the day, however, all are valuable, and can be used together to reach for the next step, the next new day, that awakening that inevitably awaits around the corner if only we are patient enough to wait for the corner to appear, and then have the courage to turn it.

## Chapter 1

# INTERNALIZING THE MESSAGES

*"Every strike brings me closer to the next home run."*
—*Babe Ruth*

**H**ow is it that we fall into the trap of confusing who we are with what we do? Do you remember the scene from "Forrest Gump" that featured Lieutenant Dan Taylor as he was recovering from a horrific injury during the Vietnam War? During the middle of a very dark night, Lieutenant Dan, now a double amputee pulls Forrest out of bed and onto the floor of the hospital. Forrest was responsible for finding, and rescuing, Lieutenant Dan during an engagement with the enemy in the jungle. He picked him up, and ran him to the helicopter, actually saving his life. It had been pointed out earlier in the movie that Lieutenant Dan came from a long line of service members in his family, and that someone had fought, and died, in every single war in the history of America. Lieutenant Dan had internalized the message that it was his destiny to do the same. Forrest had robbed him of that legacy.

The exchange that evening caught Forrest quite by surprise. In fact, he was totally unprepared by the anger Lieutenant Dan displayed. Exasperated, Lieutenant Dan screams at Forrest that he should have left him in the jungle to die. He gestures towards his legs and asks Forrest to look at him. He then asks what he is supposed to do now. He ends with a heartbreaking, "I used to be Lieutenant Dan Taylor." In all of his childlike wisdom, Forrest replies, "You are still Lieutenant Dan."

"You are still Lieutenant Dan." Think about that statement carefully. This movie scene exactly demonstrates the point I am making. When you become so enmeshed in what you do, that it overtakes your sense of who you are, you have wandered into the deep end of the pool. You have to be very careful that you have learned to swim and have figured out how to get to a lifeline to make certain you do not drown. I have nearly drowned myself. I work daily with people who are stuck in this untruth which is what you do defines who you are. When you surrender that power, you effectively have given your self-worth over to a title, a paycheck, or external recognition.

How does this happen? Look around at our society. From the earliest of ages, we are encouraged to compete, and win. I am not suggesting it is an inherently bad idea to stretch yourself to go for the trophy, title, or accolade. It is when we lose sight of the fact that it is also OK to come in second, third, or not even place. And to be able to walk away and still know our intrinsic value. The messages begin in childhood. How we are taught to deal with failure and loss is something that is vitally important. Failure is inevitable and will happen to all of us many times throughout life. It is important to develop a toolkit to address failure that is oftentimes missed. That is where the internal messaging goes off the rails, and we begin to search for excuses. The excuses are then one short step away from blame.

The blame can be shifted externally. How many times have you seen someone looking to assign the problems in their life to someone else? There is also the trap that we all fall into of getting lost in the fairness circle. Someone else gets all the breaks. No matter what you do, you cannot get ahead. There is truth to the inequity of fairness. Again, it is how we learn to deal with it that makes all the difference.

There has to be an intentional shift in the thought process to pull yourself out of the mindset that everyone else has a better lot in life than you do. It is very difficult to break old habits, especially when there are truthful examples of people getting the promotion you deserved, or the break in life you have not yet realized. At the end of the day, if you allow yourself to go down one more time than you get back up, you will not be ready when your break appears.

The blame can be shifted internally. This is where the soundtrack that we all have plays in a negative, constantly re-peating narrative. The narrative usually is filled with messages of inadequacy. Thoughts of having absolutely no control over the day-by-day, and eventually year-by-year outcome of our lives. Often, this is paired with a life that is lived in regret, looking backwards instead of ahead. I have often heard clients say things like, "Well I did it again, I am SO stupid." Or, "I can never get anything right." Another common phrase? "I do not know why I even try. Nothing is ever going to change."

When I challenge people to stop playing that soundtrack, I am often told that they are only joking around. The problem? Even if you believe you are joking, there is a part of you that is always listening. Always. If you continue to use words like, loser, stupid, dumb, and helpless, it will eventually become hardwired into your psyche. There is a lot of material out there that talks about your mindset and what happens when a negative narrative becomes the norm. What I have personally experienced and what I have seen in others is this is an absolute truth. You have to hit reset and change the narrative to positive, empowering messages.

In the worst-case scenarios I have experienced in the last twenty-five years, I have watched two colleagues lose their jobs, and never be able to hit the reset button. They began to even physically transform, as their vitality drained and they shape-shifted into a shell of who they really were. One colleague, who had made a real misstep and was fired from a prominent job eventually decided to start his car and leave the garage door closed. His family members found him the next day. All these years later, they are living with the scar of losing the person they loved and the loss of all that could have been. Another was more recent, when a young man with a jet-setting medical sales career was downsized. In this case, he had no obvious reason for being let go from the company, beyond that is the nature of the industry. As time went on and he was unable to secure another, similar position, he began to withdraw. Once again, family members found him in his home, dead from an overdose. All the potential for the future ended the day he took his life. He had internalized the wrong message, which is that what he did for a living defined his value to the world.

There is one more element that has totally compounded this type of scenario. It is the age of social media, and the constant bombardment of information. There is no quiet time, and worse yet is the inaccuracy of the information that we see on the internet and through the cycle of twenty-four hour news coverage. It is easy to internalize the message that what you are doing and what you have is not enough if you fall into the trap of comparing yourself with those images. The problem is they are often not real, or half-truths at best. Successes look glamorous as you scroll through your social media accounts. This is where we all need some real perspective. This is not just from a professional working environment, but a whole life approach.

I have been struck by the falseness and the shallowness that represents the negative side of social media. Not long ago I was in a restaurant and observed a couple endlessly taking pictures of themselves until they got just the right one to post. In the poses, they were cheek to cheek, with big smiles. The picture of happiness. The problem? As soon as the picture was posted I watched them both retreat into scrolling through their phones for the rest of the time I was there, rarely interacting with one another and all traces of their smiles gone.

Last fall, at the local pumpkin patch, I watched a young couple struggling with their small children. The kids were bickering, it was uncharacteristically hot for the fall day, and the overall picture was one of a miserable Saturday afternoon. That was real life. Over and over, the father called out for them to smile as he took pictures to post on the internet. I was astonished to watch even the smallest child, maybe just two years old, turn and freeze into a pose with a giant smile on his face. The pictures that were posted that day had absolutely no correlation whatsoever to what was actually happening in real life. It was a façade, but you would never know it unless you saw both sides.

Looking at it from a professional angle, I have clients who are posting how great their work environment is. Picture after picture of a world that seems too good to be true.

That is because it is.

The latest experience I had was when a colleague called me that I had somewhat lost touch with except through social media. By all accounts, her career was on a positive trajectory. Everything seemed to be falling into place for her and it would be easy to be a little envious. That is until you had the advantage of seeing what was on the other side of the fence. That happened for me when she called and asked to talk to me about different career paths. I was stunned when she described her CEO as, "bat-shit crazy." Again, the reality did not match the image.

I think it is very important to be judicious about how open you are with very personal aspects of your life. I also believe that the mirage painted by social media is an inadvertent downside of the technological world in which we all now live. Just be aware of it and do not let it drive your internal messaging into a downward spiral. Stay focused on you and your path. How are you going to move forward?

There is real work to be done to figure out the soundtrack in your head. Who is playing on it? What are the messages? How can you eliminate the negative ones and reinforce the positive ones?

Setting aside time for yourself to have the ability to reflect and grow personally is so important. Put yourself on your calendar and guard that time as religiously as you would guard an appointment with a colleague, boss or client. Journal. Meditate. Seek professional help to guide you if need be. I believe in mentorship and coaching as another very viable avenue to personal growth. Find someone you trust that has overcome the hurdles you see in front of you and ask them to be honest about how they navigated those same obstacles.

Sometimes the work is painful. That is ok. As long as it gets you through the valleys and back onto the higher road. Just keep going. Do you have to make peace with a parent who either intentionally or inadvertently gave you messages that you are not enough? Is there a boss in your past that treated you terribly that needs to be forgiven so you can move forward? Have you been betrayed by a friend or colleague and are still holding onto the pain? There is real truth to the premise that forgiving these people in the story of your life will actually free you. It is exhausting to drag those chains of resentment around.

Regret is also a big monster that needs to be pulled out from under the bed and sent packing. I asked myself for years how I could have been so naïve that I trusted a woman to join her in another state to be her Chief of Staff. The job turned out to be disastrous for me as I found myself reporting to someone whose moral compass in no way aligned with mine. I finally removed that monster lurking under my bed after talking it over with my mother. She asked me if I would ever treat someone the way I had been treated. When I answered no, she said, "Well, why would you have ever expected or even thought about being treated that way?" It was a simple yet profound statement. One that allowed me to stop searching for someone or something to blame and thereby spending endless energy looking back with regret.

Sometimes things just are.

I once worked with a very gifted woman who was ascending professionally, and tracking along the educational pathway to fulfill the requirements to attain her Ph.D. I was astonished when she got off track with our work together and began falling behind preparing for our coaching sessions. I pressed her for the reason. I was astonished at her response.

She shared that she had been using all her free time preparing for a presentation at a professional conference she was attending the next month. Since she was a veteran in her field, and widely recognized as a leader in her area, I asked her what could be taking so much time. From my point of view, she was a leader who could be woken from a deep sleep and would be able to speak from a point of authority about anything in her wheelhouse.

I asked if she had trouble with public speaking. She replied no. I asked if she was comfortable with the audience at that particular conference meeting. She replied yes. More perplexed than ever, I sat for a few moments in silence until she told me her truth.

"Kimberly, I am constantly researching and making new notes in the sidebar of my PowerPoint for reference. From my point of view, if someone asks a question at the end of my presentation, and I do not know the answer, then I do not have the right to be at the podium."

Wow.

Since I know that it is impossible for one human being to have the answer to every question, I began to probe. What had happened in her journey to convince her to strive for such a completely unsustainable goal?

She then shared with me that as she was growing up as a minority in America, she was told by her parents that she had to do everything better than anyone else. There is a truth to the fact that we are a long, long way from having an equitable society where minorities are given the same opportunities that the majority enjoys. Her parents were coming from a place of love, trying to equip their daughter with tools that would help her on her journey. The problem was that the message she heard and internalized was a call to arms that was completely unsustainable.

As we continued to explore this issue, she shared with me that after laboring for hours over her notes, she rarely ever referred to them in her public talks. I challenged her to approach the talk without any notes. To give herself the gift of getting comfortable with one simple phrase. That phrase?

"I do not know."

No one can know everything. Getting comfortable with acknowledging that there is a question that you cannot answer is not only honest and freeing, it allows everyone else the grace to follow that example. The trick is to know where to find the information, and then be sure to give feedback later.

This particular woman accepted my challenge. She approached that podium absent her extensive notes and conquered the presentation. She effectively rewrote the narrative that had been playing since her childhood that she had to be better than anyone else or she would not be successful.

There are all sorts of tools, and techniques that you can find to break the cycle of negative messaging. My favorite? I often ask my clients to wear a rubber band around their wrist and simply snap it when the negative soundtrack starts. It may sound silly, but I can personally attest that it has worked for me and many people I have coached. It is organizing in the way that kicking your toe on the nightstand is. It gets your attention and it puts you back in conscious control of the messages you are sending yourself. You are enough. Everyone falls. How can you grow from the experience? What is next? If you allow yourself to step back far enough to gain real perspective, you can even have some fun.

## Chapter 2

# LOSING THE WAY

*"Most of the shadows of this life are caused*
*by our standing in our own sunshine."*
*—Ralph Waldo Emerson*

**D**o you remember the first time you were hired? No matter what age, or what level the position was, do you remember the feeling of accomplishment? Whether hired on the spot, a phone call, an email, or text, connect back to that rush of positivity. You were chosen.

In the beginning, most of us package ourselves and begin to sell that package to potential employers. We think we have a clear idea of who we are and begin to target those employers that can benefit from our talents. Sometimes we pursue positions that are stepping-stones along the educational pathway. Positions that sustain us as we pursue dreams. No matter the position, there is an inherent sense of pride when the offer is extended. There is a real sense of accomplishment that comes when we can earn money and begin the journey of self-reliance.

Knowing who we are is key to this process. The problems start when we begin to pay less attention to who we are than to what we do. When we give all of ourselves over to the role and the position begins to redefine how we think about ourselves.

It is a tricky balancing act. It is positive to be proud of accomplishments in the workplace. It is a good thing to be the very best you can be at whatever work you do. Pushing forward and striving for excellence are all positive attributes. It is when those tip over and become pitfalls that the struggle begins. It is when we begin to think about ourselves as Lieutenant Dan, instead of Dan that we become most vulnerable.

This happens at every level of the workforce. I have seen CEOs and presidents who simply transform into the worst possible version of themselves when they are entrusted with the top job. They appear to have forgotten who they are and seem oblivious to the harm they inflict on the organization and their employees when they behave badly.

One warning sign is when someone becomes overly attentive to titles. I was in a meeting where the CEO had just introduced his new finance director to the executive team. The new director had known the CEO for years as his wife had tutored the CEO's children. The director had been at the CEO's house for holidays and the families had grown quite close. When the new director was asked to share a little bit about himself, he referred to the CEO by first name. The CEO leaned over to his secretary and whispered. She grew very uncomfortable.

The CEO prompted her again, and she interrupted the director mid-sentence. She then directed him to address the CEO by his formal title going forward. The director looked absolutely mortified. He never quite fully recovered, stammering his way through the remainder of his remarks, and then thanked the CEO by his formal title for the opportunity to join the company.

The director never did regain his footing, and never was able to find his way successfully at the company after such a stilted beginning. The CEO had sandbagged any chance of him not being the fodder for gossip in the hallways. What had happened, exactly?

The CEO had lost his way. He had confused his title and position with who he was as a human being. I imagine if he had the opportunity to see how he had acted played back for him on video he would have cringed at his behavior. He had become so tied up in what he was doing, he always needed those titles and accolades to feel worthy. As a result, he had crippled a talented employee before they could even get off the ground.

There are many opportunities to lose the way. Sometimes it is being consumed by watching too closely what others are doing and not paying enough attention to your pathway. Comparison can be healthy when it is focused on positives such as emulating a mentor who is a support and has achieved what you aspire to become. It becomes unhealthy when it is a scoreboard that is kept. This leads to harboring feelings of being overlooked or left behind.

I am not suggesting that advocating for oneself should ever be swept aside. The reality is that there will be many, many instances where circumstances are unfair. In the worst circumstances, they may even be illegal. It is important to stand up and fight the fights that need fighting.

What I am referring to is the thought processes that lead to behaviors that self-sabotage efforts to move ahead in a healthy manner. Losing the way can be a result of reaching for the title or position at all costs. These include sabotaging others, sacrificing morals and principles and lying to yourself that the end defends the means.

There is a big difference in being competitive and being deceptive. Lying to yourself or others is always a huge red flag. Undermining or lying about others is another. Pulling people down instead of focusing on raising yourself up is a classic example of losing the way. Why are we so terrified that someone else will get ahead of us?

The underpinning of losing the way is forgetting who you are. Why did you begin the journey in the first place? It is important to always be able to tap into the joy of the work that you are doing, and remember it is separate than the person that you are. Whatever position you hold is inevitably for a finite period. You have been entrusted with the role and whatever power it holds. How will history retell what you did with your turn?

A positive example of separating who you are with your title and what you do rests with a university president I know. He arrived at a conference and as he was checking in, he was handed his nametag. It had his credentials listed, including his formal first name, not the one he preferred to go by. I watched in amazement as he thanked the clerk for the nametag and asked if he could borrow a black marker. He then slid the paper out of his lanyard and crossed out the name and title so fully you could not read it. He then wrote beneath it, "Jim."

He turned to me and noticed I was watching. He smiled and simply said, "My name is Jim. Not Dr."

Clearly, a leader who had a very healthy understanding of the delineation between what he did and who he was. In this instance, he was using who he was to influence how he was behaving as he operated in his role.

I later had the opportunity to speak with him about that day. He went on to share with me that he believed that people should be able to understand who you are by how you carry yourself and treat others. I have carried that sentiment from that day to this.

People should be able to know who you are by the way that you treat them. This is universal.

Losing your way can also occur when you allow negative messages to begin and continue to play. So many people who have worked hard and been recognized and promoted begin to doubt themselves. When fear takes hold, there is usually a negative outcome. The only good example I can think of relative to fear is when it warns you that there is a Velociraptor behind the next tree and you need to run to save your life! Otherwise, fear that you do not belong, you are not good enough, you do not deserve what you have usually leads to circling the drain.

People who become fearful often lose their way because their thinking becomes clouded with all the "what-ifs" they can conceive of. "What if I fail?" "What if I cannot go to the podium without trembling?" "What if I am not supposed to be here?"

These are all tenants of, The Imposter Syndrome. The fear that drives this syndrome will definitely cause you to lose your way. Often, fear will cause people to become the worst versions of themselves. In the aftermath, it can cause terrible consequences, for not only the person but the organization as well. The organization is comprised of real people, with real lives that can be destroyed.

Leaders need to be very careful about another pitfall that will definitely lead them into the deep end of the ocean. It can begin innocently enough. Becoming clouded in your thinking between who you are and what you do can lead to making irresponsible decisions.

Leaders of organizations need to always strive to be fair, empathetic, supportive, empowering, the list of positives goes on. They need to be friendly. They need to completely separate that from the idea of being friends with those they lead. I saw this mistake cost a president his role at a public university.

The president had gotten quite close personally to an employee that was at the university when he took the helm. The employee was not producing at a professional level. Worse yet, he was vindictive, and undermined everyone around him. Instead of staying the course and keeping a professional boundary, the new president crossed that line and ended up in a personal space with the employee. The men were seen having lunch and clapping one another on the back. In short order the president elevated the employee to an interim role on his executive team. Alarm bells began to sound around the campus. The judgement of the president was questioned. The president had not done the work to build bridges and lay a foundation of trust with the faculty and staff, so most were too fearful to directly question him. Those that did found him to be unreceptive at best.

Before long, the employee was offered the role permanently. He often showed up late and left early for meetings. He was explosive and abusive in his new role. He actually was rarely on campus for a whole day. As more departments were moved under his new role, he began to travel extensively. He had a policy that he attended any conference that any of his direct reports attended. Budgets became strained. The president refused to intervene. Eventually there were trips that the president and employee attended together. The problem? There was very little to show for the money spent on the trips. Resentment began to grow.

Whenever someone did stand up to the abusive employee, they found themselves in the crosshairs of his wrath. The president turned a blind eye. It all culminated one day when there was a misunderstanding on campus. It spun into a crisis due to the lack of leadership on the part of the president. The president was also following very bad advice. The employee was instrumental in recommending that the president terminate a colleague that he did not like. The president did, releasing a high-performing member of the team, while continuing to ignore the multitude of issues the employee he had elevated was causing.

As the truth became known, those whom the president reported to began to investigate. The investigation revealed the inequities that existed in the expectations set by the president for his direct reports. When the budget was examined, there was simply no explanation for allowing so much funding to be appropriated for the negative employee's constant travelling. The absenteeism of the employee also came to light, along with the abusive way he managed his departments. Before long, the president submitted a letter of resignation, and the employee was asked to leave not long afterwards. At the end of the day, they had harmed themselves, but even worse, the university and all the stakeholders that were there.

Losing the way can also come at the hands of those who elevate people into positions without ever training them as to what leadership looks like. Many people think that leadership is about telling others what to do. In actuality, leadership is much more about empathy, integrity and listening than directing others. Learning how to use your influence in a positive way to effect change is so important. That can only happen with a healthy self-awareness, so you know where you stand and what you stand for. Then you use your power. And you use it for the good as you cast a vision for your subordinates. A lot of listening needs to happen when you find yourself in a position of leadership. Empowering your team and then giving them deserved praise is another tenant of successful leadership.

A concrete example that I have seen many times over lies in the medical community. Often, in the medical imaging arena, a technologist will rise to prominence as a star. They are excellent at working with patients. In the examination rooms, they can operate independently and make swift decisions. The results are outstanding. Patients are well cared for and the star technologist continues to progress and evolve professionally.

The error that has happened is when management makes the mistake in elevating the star technologist to a position managing the department without additional education and training. The star technologist is placed into the new role and problems inevitably arise. Why?

It is two completely different skill sets to be successful as a star technologist versus a successful manager. As a technologist, one is operating almost entirely independently, and likely swiftly as critical decisions about patient care emerge. The technologist is not required to meet with teams. They are a technical expert and doing their best work when they are interacting with their patient. Once they become a department manager, almost the opposite skill set is required to be successful. They must slow down to consider their entire team's needs. They must work collaboratively up and down the entire chain of command as a link in the management chain. They have to communicate and be able to lead team meetings to a positive outcome. Often this may mean dealing with employees who are unhappy about issues. Managing people is very different than managing as an independent technologist working directly with patient care. It can lead to a very negative outcome if there is not a purposeful intervention to provide the additional training for the technologist. The worst-case scenario is that the technologist resigns their new role as a manager. This leaves the organization with two big vacancies: the management position as well as the vacated star technologist position.

The stakes are so high with regard to safeguarding against losing the way. It takes work, faith, hope, and clear goals to ensure that you do not get lost. It also takes courage. Courage becomes even more important when you are faced with someone who is actively working against you, encouraging you off the positive pathway. That is when trust has to kick in. Trust in who, or what? That is the best kept secret I have ever learned. Trust in yourself, and who you are. It is the only way to either not lose your way or rebound. If, like most of us, you do lose your way, that trust in yourself, coupled with courage, faith and hope will lead you back. It is not an automatic rebound. You must be purposeful and determined to be successful.

In 2008, I was feeling the effects of the economy bottoming out. For me, though, it was also compounded with other losses. I was struggling with how to find my way back to the light after life took many negative turns. On my birthday that next year, my mother gave me a card that first sat on my desk, and later I framed. It hangs on my wall to this day. The author is not listed, so I cannot give credit to whomever wrote it. It has helped me for more than a decade to recalibrate whenever I feel like I am losing my way.

*How to Make a Beautiful Life*
*Reflection for a Daughter on her Birthday*

*Love yourself.*
*MAKE PEACE with who you are at this moment in time.*

*Listen to your heart.*
*If you can't hear what it's saying in this noisy world,*
*MAKE TIME for yourself.*
*Enjoy your own company.*
*Let your mind wander among the stars.*

*Try.*
*Take chances.*

*MAKE MISTAKES.*
*Life can be messy and confusing at times,*
*but it's also full of surprises.*
*The next rock in your path might be a stepping-stone.*

*Be happy.*
*When you don't have what you want, want what you have.*
*MAKE DO.*
*That's a well-kept secret of contentment.*

*There aren't any shortcuts to tomorrow.*
*You have to MAKE YOUR OWN WAY.*
*To know where you're going is only part of it.*
*You need to know where you've been, too.*
*And if you ever get lost, don't worry.*
*The people who love you will find you.*
*Count on it.*

*Life isn't days and years.*
*It's what you do with time and all the*
*goodness and grace that's inside you.*
*MAKE A BEAUTIFUL LIFE....*
*The kind of life you deserve.*

We all deserve a beautiful life. When you lose your way, take a breath. With a deliberate plan, there is a pathway back, and then forward.

## Chapter 3

# THERE IS NO STRAIGHT LINE

---

*"We have to do the best we can. This is
our sacred human responsibility."*
—*Albert Einstein*

**W**e can get very distracted by life. Most of us begin by
believing that things will progress in a straight line.

The reality is that life does not actually work that way. No
matter what plans we make, no matter how carefully we tend
to those plans, life does not lay itself out in a straight line. It
comes in fits and starts. Our reaction to both the positive and
negative turns that our lives take along the way determines how
we ultimately manage what comes our way.

Know this. Every minute that you spend investing in yourself
and your truth will help to build the foundation that is necessary
to sustain you through both the high points and the valleys. You

must spend time understanding your line in the sand. What do I mean by this?

What are your non-negotiables? Realize that these will certainly shift over your lifetime. As your experiences shape you, it is only natural for your value system to grow and evolve.

What I experienced personally, and now experience daily with those I work with, is the value in understanding personal non-negotiables. I had not done that sort of work myself until the bottom dropped out. For me, I was in the middle of a crisis and trying to understand my own moral compass. It left me doing the proverbial building the plane while trying to learn how to fly. This did not serve me well, and I certainly do not recommend it.

I often refer to investing in this process by comparing it to attending driving school. Have you ever been offered the chance to go to driving school versus having points added to your license, which will raise your insurance rate? After being pulled over for speeding?

That happened to me, and I was sitting through the class that winter evening listening to the instructor talk about what to do if you find yourself in the midst of a loss of control of your car. I remember so clearly him describing that so many times people panic and do not even realize they are holding their breath and closing their eyes as a result of the trauma of the incident taking place. I listened, received my certificate, and then left.

It was not two weeks before I found myself in a spin out on I-75 north after attending a professional luncheon in Lexington, KY. It was in December and I was in a sports car that had only two seats. The unpredicted storm left a terrifying coat of black ice all over the highway.

It felt like a scene out of a movie as it happened so quickly, but also felt like it was going in slow motion at the same time. I was not travelling very fast, as it was obvious that there was black ice all over the highway. I still do not know what set the series of events off, but I found myself starting into a spin and there was absolutely nothing I could do to prevent it. Suddenly I heard the driving school instructor's voice in my head. He suggested screaming if necessary to ensure you keep breathing. I clearly remembered his instruction to not close my eyes and to steer into the turn instead of what seems more natural, which is to steer out of it.

I did three full revolutions and each time I was facing the wrong direction I could see the traffic heading my way. I found myself in the slow lane, facing completely backwards and looking at a terrified truck driver who was clearly unable to stop as his eighteen-wheeler continued to head towards me. I believe it was both an act of God and the training I had just been through that changed the outcome of that terrible event.

I was breathing, watching, and continuing to steer into the slide when suddenly my steering wheel began to be of use to me. I was able to turn back in the right direction and then navigate into the safety lane on the side of the road. The outcome changed in a few seconds from very bleak to avoiding the accident altogether.

Preparing for a wreck, whether it is on the roadway or in your personal or professional life, is time very well spent. Just as the driving school helped prepare me to steer my way to safety, taking time to identify and then respond to your line in the sand will serve you well.

The straight line you set yourself upon takes unusual turns. Sometimes you can see the ninety-degree turn approaching and feel powerless to stop it. Other times, you may be totally blind-sided by a ninety, or even one-hundred-eighty-degree turn. It can be quite disempowering if you do not figure out how to steer into the storm and ultimately retake control.

No matter where you are on your pathway, it is critical that you take time to do your own internal inventory. It begins with identifying where you ultimately draw your personal line in the sand. It takes work to understand what building blocks are the foundation for that decision. Breaking those blocks down makes it easier to understand. Do not get overwhelmed with the process. Simply make a commitment to begin it and then honor that commitment.

Journaling is a powerful tool to navigate through the process. Journaling does not have to be long written notes. It can be bullets, pictures, fragments of sentences, anything that helps to organize your thoughts.

Often the straight line goes off track because we find ourselves in a situation where our moral compass is being violated. You will inevitably get lost along the way if you have not spent the time to understand what is happening, and where your moral compass lies.

Moral injury is a concept that is fairly well researched, but not very well understood. By definition, moral injury refers to the condition that occurs when people are exposed to suffering that occurs in situations where high stakes are involved. For our purposes, I am going to focus specifically on situations that are connected to your ability to earn a living. Being placed into an environment where you must choose between what you believe and know is wrong to do or face being released from your job if you refuse to do it lead to moral injury. From the outside it can look very easy. Is it wrong? Quit! Take a stand. However, when you step back and consider the storm that is happening it becomes easy to understand that it is not a black or white answer. It can become very muddled. It has so many, many shades of grey.

When this happened to me, I found myself at a stage in my life where I was a single mother, and terrified of losing my income. After all, if I went down, I was not going down alone. I was taking my youngest daughter with me. As I travelled through the pathway of moral injury, I experienced all the now known symptoms. Shame. Guilt. Self-condemnation. I was furious. I was utterly lost.

At the time, I had not done the work to understand what my moral boundaries were, and I had no idea what other options were present. I felt literally, and completely, trapped.

What I did not understand at the time was that the trappings were more of my own making than of my boss. Moral injury can be triggered by something that we did, something that was done to us, or something that we have seen. For me, it was a combination of all three.

I had made the decision to accept the invitation to take a fatal job offer. That was something I did. I was mistreated when I was serving in the role. That was something that happened to me. I saw others mistreated at the hands of the administration. That was something I witnessed. At the lowest point, I was instructed to lead the efforts to mistreat a colleague. It was infuriating, terrifying, and tested me to my very core. I knew I did not agree with what was happening to myself and others. What was less clear was how to steer my way out of the storm. I did not know basic things like my financial bottom line, and options. I was totally unequipped to handle the emotional turmoil that came along with the situation in which I found myself. I spent far too much time in self-condemnation to allow enough energy to appoint to a solution. I was in a very confusing place. Since that dark time, I have encountered so many others who have suffered moral injury and are lost as well.

One breakthrough that occurred for me was when I found the benefit of journaling. I began to understand how organizing, and empowering journaling was. It helped me to keep track of my wild thoughts that were under siege as I travelled that road. It gave me a starting point each day as I reviewed what I had written the day before. It helped me begin to understand trends and patterns so I could identify a way forward, which helped me to go in a different direction. A direction that I was controlling.

Let me underscore that I understand the aversion many have to journaling. So many of the clients I work with either silently or even audibly groan when I suggest journaling. What has been surprising to me is that those who groan the most loudly are the ones who find journaling the most satisfying. They fill up the journal I give them, writing up and down the margins on the pages, and then buy another journal to continue. It will pay off with dividends. Here's why:

Journaling can begin with spending time making forced choices about what is most important to you. What values do you hold dear? Again, values can certainly shift over the course of a lifetime, but the hard and fast ones will remain. Do you value service to others? Recognition? The ability to contribute? Ethical behavior? Begin to do a deep dive into this issue to start to narrow down your core value system. Write it down and spend time contemplating why they are meaningful to you. Where did they come from? Which ones are absolute? Once you identify which ones are the most meaningful, you will be a step closer to knowing where your line in the sand falls.

Why is this so important? If a turn in the road finds you matched with a job that violates your moral compass, it is important to understand how far it has to go before you find yourself standing with your toes on that line. What will you do? Some violate their principles and begin to act in ways that are against their moral value system. This can be for a multitude of reasons, the least of which is the fear of losing their job.

Losing a job has real consequences. Immediately there are concerns around financial requirements and how to take care of yourself and anyone else who depends on you. There can be a stigma attached as you search for a job while unemployed.

It goes deeper than that, though. Many of us will begin to circle the drain, searching for reasons why the road turned. All the negative monsters begin to surface. Blame. Regret. Reliving decisions from long ago.

I promise the problem will also be confounded if you violate your moral compass for the sake of a job. I have worked with people who have said they did not recognize themselves in the mirror anymore.

The worst scenario? Violating your moral compass and performing in ways that you normally would not and being fired from your job anyway. When you find yourself aligned with an organization that behaves in unethical ways, or reporting to a leader who is morally compromised, you must make clear decisions. That task is exasperated because the pressure is very real for the person caught in the cross hairs. Betrayal is a huge factor in this process. Most of the time, the work began with the usual celebratory activities associated with a new job. Trying to figure out how everything fell apart can be exhausting. Sometimes you can look back and realize that there were people along the pathway that were rooting for you to fail. That sense of betrayal is brutal and runs very deep. During my personal crisis, I made the decision to head to a new state to take a new role with a brand-new leader. My mentor wisely cautioned me to be aware of the Weebees. I did not know what a Weebee was. Something unique to the state?

The answer? "Kimberly, the Weebees are those who will not like the change you are being charged to lead and will take the following stand: We've been here before you arrived, we will be here when we run you off."

It was prophetic.

Knowing where you are willing and able to compromise your values and where you absolutely cannot is a very valuable block of knowledge. It is only when you are clear on this that you can begin to search effectively for employers who are aligned with your beliefs.

Identify your ethical questions. What are they, exactly? Where do your ethics play into the overall picture of your life? As you identify those ethical questions buckle up to answer them. One of the fundamental questions is who are you? What do you want? What moral line do you know and identify with and will ultimately hold fast? Have you stepped over that line? How do you know? What led to that situation?

Employers, listen carefully. This process not only is valuable for individuals to complete. It is vital for organizations to also examine the culture that is being cultivated. If the organization is allowed to deteriorate into a climate of fear and distrust, the talent you will attract will certainly reflect it. Setting the tone from the very top is essential.

As you follow your ethical and moral compass there are two pathways to consider.

What is the outcome if you do nothing?

What is the outcome if you take a stand?

There are two very different eventualities that happen when you follow your truth. There is a price that is attached to both.

There is a price that you pay whether you follow your moral compass or whether you ignore it. Make no mistake about it.

If you do not follow your moral compass, the price you pay is often a life that is riddled with pain and conflict. That is because you know the right thing to do, but do not do it. All the negative emotions that ensue can be crippling. Shame at not doing what you believe is right. Outrage that you have been put in such a situation to begin with. Sorrow as you try to figure out how things went so far off the rails. Resentment of others who appear to have it all together. Disbelief at how it all fell apart.

If you do follow your moral compass it usually involves taking a brave stand. Sometimes this finds people acting as whistle-blowers. Often it can mean that you act in ways that are defined by management as insubordination. Refusing to follow orders to do something you believe is wrong can quickly find you ostracized and left outside the circle. Scarier still? More often than not, organizations with deep pockets circle the wagons, even when they know the employee speaking out is correct.

I find this phenomenon very hard to understand. But I also know that it is the default position in most of these types of situations. I have seen organizations spend literally millions of dollars defending an indefensible position. When you step forward to sound the alarm, you must understand that you need to have the grit and determination to see it through.

When I found myself in this situation, I finally did decide to take a stand. I reached out to a mentor who I greatly respected. She had taken a stand years before when she was faced with a situation in her workplace that was not only wrong. It was unconscionable. She had been accused of embezzlement after serving a quarter of a century in service to her employer. She was recognized widely as a leader to be emulated and had earned many community service awards. The news that hit the media was shocking and tantalizing and spread like wildfire.

The problem was it was totally untrue. When the accounting error finally surfaced to prove that she had, in fact, done no wrong whatsoever, there was a turn of events that illustrates my point. Instead of falling on their sword, and apologizing and making things right, management doubled down and refused to reinstate her, and continued to deny her access to her retirement benefits.

For seven years. They doubled down for seven long years.

During all that time, the cost to the organization was astronomical. She followed her lawyer's advice and finally sued. The outcome was a trial that resulted in her favor. Besides being reinstated and awarded her earned retirement benefits, the organization was also ordered to pay her attorney's fees as well as big dollars for all she had been through.

As I was determining which path I would go down, I called my mentor. I felt my life was a total ball of confusion. I will never forget her advice to me. "Kimberly, you figure out what it will take to make this right for you, and then you hire a good lawyer and tell them to go get it."

I remember sharing that I did not know how to handle all the swirling rumors and the cruel behavior from the organization I had formerly been associated with. Her answer? "You don't care." I remember squeaking out a response that I really did care. She reiterated, "You know who you are, you know what happened. You don't care. Stand firm and make this right for yourself. Decide what you need to make this situation right, find a lawyer you respect and tell them to go get it for you."

There are so many organizations that are examples of treating employees with dignity and respect. Conversely, there are many that do not. Finding yourself working for one of these organizations can take you off your straight line in short order.

I worked with an organization that had a leader who was quite dysfunctional and cruel. He oversaw a company that had a headquarters in Florida, and satellite sites scattered across the country all the way to Hawaii. His leadership team were people he recruited that were lock step with his way of thinking and managing. They often retreated into secret meetings, and when they emerged, there were decisions made that were final and often negatively affected many employees. I remember an instance where a few new employees were invited out to a celebratory lunch at the end of their first week. Several of those employees had already begun to figure out that the culture of the organization was not what they were led to believe or had hoped. At the luncheon, a senior vice president encouraged the new employees to leave the lunch and simply go home early for the weekend. When one of the employees remarked they needed to go back to the office to finish a few things the suggestion changed to a directive. Why? The leader shared with the new folks that several of the office mates they had just met were being informed that they were no longer needed at the company and were in the process of being escorted out of the office that afternoon. No notice. No legitimate reason. Simply the culture of the organization.

I attempted to work with the president to explain that people were terrified every day they came to work. The terror was interfering with work performance and causing all kinds of stress. The worst day of the week was always Friday. Instead of it being the day before the weekend with all the employees making plans with family and friends, everyone was quaking in their boots. Everyone was waiting for a meeting to inform him or her that it was his or her last day. Sometimes, it was whole satellites who would read at 4:45 p.m. that effective at 5:00 p.m. their satellite was being closed, and the entire staff would be let go. When I shared the effect I had learned from every direction that this was having on the morale and physical, psychological, and emotional health of his staff the president smiled. I was perplexed and said, "Your employees are scared to death." His response? "That is just the way I want it."

Why? Of course, there are examples of bad actors that are in powerful positions. Oftentimes, I have discovered other reasons. One of the biggest is a person who is out of touch with themselves and who possesses a tone-deafness for the needs of those around them. There is also the plain and simple bad manager who has internalized all the wrong lessons about what strong management looks like. The result invariably is that in this type of environment talent will leave. Those who have opportunities to pursue other avenues will do just that. Which leaves an already dysfunctional organization with all their best employees exiting, thereby weakening the company further.

That is exactly what happened with this particular organization.

Transparency and honesty are qualities that are essential to cultivate a work environment that is healthy, and attracts and retains top talent. There are so many examples to look to as leaders in this area.

During the disastrous economic crash of 2008, many organizations found themselves searching for answers to balance their bottom line. Everyone was aware of the consequences of losing their jobs during this tumultuous time.

The leadership of Northern Kentucky University set about balancing the budget for the upcoming fiscal year. Committing to transparency, the president held public forums to explain the process and field questions. The budget was examined line by line and difficult decisions were considered. Finally, the day arrived where it was apparent that in order to keep the university solvent, furloughs would be necessary.

The president once again honored the commitment to transparency and went to the constituents to discuss timelines and how Human Resources would be handling cuts. There were many facets to the plan that included early retirements and not refilling vacancies from employees who departed for other reasons. He shared that there was a great deal of resources in the plan to transition anyone who would eventually be furloughed. Additionally, the release dates were set in the future, allowing for employees to look for other opportunities. There were many areas of support such as career counseling offered.

The result? Morale improved across the campus. Faculty and staff felt secure in the leadership and had a deep sense of trust in the information that had been shared. No one wasted valuable energy worrying that their livelihood would be taken from them without notice. As a result, the organization continued to serve its mission. As time went along the people affected by the cuts found pathways to other places. Loyalty to the university swelled.

During the COVID-19 crisis another type of challenge arose that was unique. It was quite literally overnight that orders came in from the state level to shutter businesses in order to contain the novel virus. It was a turn in the road that was unprecedented. Some business leaders panicked and made decisions that were crippling to their employees and those they served.

Clovernook Center for the Blind and Visually Impaired did exactly the opposite. A great deal of time had already been invested in defining the core values of the organization prior to the onset of the pandemic. They had defined their culture and communicated it to all the stakeholders. Since they knew what their ethical foundation was built upon prior to the crisis, no time had to be invested in figuring out where they stood.

The leadership came together to construct a plan to deal with the crisis. They used transparency and honesty to convey their plan. Long before all the government relief aid was announced, the leadership made a commitment to continue to pay all their employees who were under stay at home orders. They did not want the additional stress of wondering if a paycheck was coming in to further exacerbate the uncertain future.

Once the stay at home orders were lifted, the leadership communicated that they would accommodate anyone who felt the need to continue to work remotely and phase coming back in stages. They understood that their employees were real people facing real issues. Working together, the organization protected both its interests and its personnel.

The result was everyone found themselves protected and cared for. The organization both employs and serves individuals who are blind or visually impaired. This protected population found a support mechanism in Clovernook, which helped them through the crisis rather than further harmed by it.

It is a familiar mantra that is worth repeating: leadership matters.

Whatever turn in the road takes you off a straight line, it will be far easier to navigate with foundational work that has been completed so you know exactly where your ethical lines fall. This is true for individuals at every level of the workforce. It is also true for leadership as they define the culture of their organization. Investing in the process will serve you well when the unexpected shows up. Get this work done. Purposefully set time aside to do it. Keep at it. Once you are successful in doing the work for at least 28 days, it will become a new habit.

Know that the work is never completed. As we all evolve and continue down the pathway, core values will invariably shift. Staying abreast of what is most important to you from an ethical standpoint will ensure that you are driving the train. This is far better than being run over by it when it comes through.

A fun yet organizing activity that helps to clarify where you have been and where you are going is to draw your lifeline. Take a sheet of paper and draw a line on it from one end to the other. On the left-hand side draw a hash mark and label it zero. On the right-hand side draw a hash mark and label it one-hundred. Assume your lifespan is going to be one-hundred years. Begin by populating your line with hash marks that denote your most important landmarks. Really give this some introspective thought. The landmarks should reflect both positive and negative events. Are any patterns revealed? Most importantly, look at the timeline that remains beginning from today. What do you want to accomplish? Did the activities you have invested in gotten you farther down the pathway towards your goals, or have they derailed your progress? What needs to happen next? Who do you need to pull into the conversation to support your efforts? Who do you need to eliminate? What is activity that is valuable versus activity that is distracting you? How do you know?

Reclaim your power and take one step at a time towards your goals. Create the life that you want.

## Chapter 4

# WHAT REALLY WORKS?

*"Whatever you can do, or dream you can, begin it.*
*Boldness has genius, power and magic in it."*
—*Johann Wolfgang von Goethe*

What really works? You must do the work to identify your value system, where your moral compass truly lies, and therefore your drop-dead line in the sand. Beyond that, the people you surround yourself with are crucial.

It is so important to understand who is in your support system when the straight line you are on makes either a dreaded expected turn, or a turn that is totally not on your radar. There are people who will surprise you and step up to be supportive. Unfortunately, there are people you have trusted who will step back.

It is a strange phenomenon that people will distance themselves from someone who is in a valley. It is almost as if they will catch the negative circumstances if they stand firm. It is very stressful to go through a negative situation that finds you out of work. It is likewise stressful to see those you know and care about go through it.

The best advice I have is to locate those people who you know will show up for you. The people in your circle with whom you have open, honest communication that you can count on. You need those who will have crucial conversations with you in every area of life, but especially during a crisis.

One way to identify who those people are is quite simple. Search for empathetic responses to your questions and problems from those you let into your innermost circle. Sometimes, quite by mistake, people will try to fix things for you by making statements that are not helpful. At my lowest point, I turned to a friend and was shocked by her response: "I am not going to sugarcoat it for you, Kimberly. I do not believe you are ever going to work again."

There was almost a gleeful tone when she made the statement. I physically stepped backwards even though she was on the phone and not in front of me. To help me sort this out I talked with my minister. He had insight that I found very helpful.

He believes that there are some people who only know how to be your friend and support you when you are doing well. Conversely, he believes that there are others who only know how to be your friend and support you when you are on your knees. He suggested that I simply tighten my circle and remove the people who fell into those categories.

The most valuable support system you can build is with those who will simply sit with you. Whether you are celebrating or down in a dark well of despair, they will sit with you. There are times when those people have valuable insight and wisdom to share. Oftentimes, they may not know what to say, but are comfortable sitting with you anyway. Those are the people you want in your squad.

One of the best qualities your support system brings to the table is accountability. When life throws you a curve ball, you need those who will check in with you and make sure you are doing alright. It is natural to take time to grieve when there is a loss of a job. Loss is profound throughout life. You simply cannot allow yourself to go down into the depths of grief and get stuck there. To quote a Japanese proverb: "Fall seven times and stand up eight."

The key is to not get stuck. Accountability partners can be enormously helpful with this. When I was struggling after the loss of a job, my thoughts began to spiral out of control. I was several years down the road into the future imagining all sorts of horrendous scenarios. One of my accountability partners simply said, "Remember nothing is going to change today. You are not going to be homeless today."

It allowed me to free myself from those chains and redirect that energy. I began to be purposeful about planning for the future versus being terrified of it. I found that once I turned that corner, the fear became less and less. In fact, I have never been as afraid again of the uncertainties that lie ahead.

One very beneficial thing to do with an unexpected pause due to a job loss is to invest time in self-discovery. There are several assessments that are readily available. Two of my favorites are the DiSC and the NSight Success Assessment.

DiSC is a test based on four personality traits. It is fast and easy to take. The results will reveal what basic behavioral tendencies you lean on, especially in times of crisis. DiSC is an acronym that stands for:

D = The Dominance Tendency: People who fall into this tendency want immediate results and can be risk-takers.

i = The Influence Tendency: People who fall into this tendency are very people-oriented and can be impulsive.

S = The Steadiness Tendency: People who fall into this tendency prefer consistency and can resist change.

C = The Conscientiousness Tendency: People who fall into this tendency prefer attention to detail and can be resistant to delegation of work.

You can fall into more than one tendency. Knowing what your tendency is can help you map your way to a new professional opportunity that will fall in alignment with it. As I shared before, we turn to our tendencies even more frequently when we are under stress. It is natural to feed our strengths. Knowing what they are allows you to spend time in personal development to address your weaknesses. We all have them. Recognizing what they are is a powerful tool in your toolkit.

The NSight Success Assessment is a little longer than the DiSC. This assessment tool also measures personality traits and behavioral styles but goes further by assessing aptitude. It pulls the information into the following dimensions: Self-Perception, Thinking Style, Drive, Stress, Communication, Leadership and Reliability. NSight illuminates areas that fall into extreme scores, allowing you to not only raise your awareness but also develop a plan to address areas that may be pitfalls. Are you an emotional decision-maker? Someone who freezes when pressure is applied? Someone who avoids confrontation at all costs? Spending time to gain a deeper self-knowledge will pay great dividends as you prepare for upcoming professional opportunities.

Navigating your way through self-assessments can be performed on your own, but if you really want to drill down find a coach who can guide you. Identifying a coach needs to be done with as much thoughtfulness and care as identifying mentors. It must be a good fit on both sides. Do not be shy about voicing your feeling that a particular coach is not a good match for you. You may be surprised when interviewing coaches that one may share they do not think it is a good fit. If the relationship does not click at the beginning, all the work that comes afterwards will be less than optimal.

Coaches help with guiding you through self-assessments, but there is so much more to gain from that formalized relationship. Coaches are inherently bound to be accountability partners. They can help you peel back layers of defensiveness that allow you to examine your journey to date and help guide you along purposeful planning for forging ahead.

Another benefit a coach offers is assisting you with setting the stage for holding the crucial conversations you need to have as you heal from the trauma of a job loss. Make no mistake about it. It is traumatic. You may find yourself having difficulty communicating to others what happened. You may internalize the issue and have trouble rebounding. Finding safe spaces to talk through these issues is paramount to moving forward. A good coach can help you span those barriers and foster honest conversations. This is accomplished by creating psychologically safe environments in which to conduct them.

By definition, psychological safety is where you very intentionally create an environment of trust and inclusion. It fosters communication and does not allow personal vitriol at any level. This creates an atmosphere that encourages spirited debate that allows for positive outcomes.

Part of the equation for success is getting comfortable with dissonance. When a high level of trust is established within the relationship of the person or people with whom you are holding crucial conversations, dissonance is more comfortable. You want honest feedback. Sometimes that feedback is uncomfortable. The goal is to create a safe space in which to receive it so you can move through it and grow.

In facilitating psychologically safe environments, a good coach will encourage you to learn from failures. There is no human being who is free from failure. To quote Michael Jordan: "I've missed more than 9000 shots in my career. I've lost almost 300 games. 26 times I've been trusted to take the game winning shot and missed. I've failed over and over and over again in my life. And that is why I succeed."

It is so critical that you turn failure on its head and look at it as what it really is. Failure is a teacher with opportunity that lies on the other side of the valley. Keep your discussions about failure focused. Populate your support circle with those who agree to your psychologically safe boundaries.

Another exercise that really works in the journey of self-discovery is one that I use titled, *Why Am I Afraid To Tell You Who I Am?* It is powerful and involves deep introspection and journaling. I have used it personally, one-on-one with clients, as well as in large group settings. Here is how it works. You put time on your calendar and honor it to work on this step. Then start to jot down responses to the prompt. Examples I have received have run the gamut. In group settings, I often take up the responses and read them to ensure anonymity.

When someone has come through a job loss, there is often the fear of stigma that they will never escape. Some examples I have received from people in this category are:

- "I am afraid to tell you that I have been fired before and you will not think I am employable."
- "I am afraid to tell you that I have battled an addiction and you will think I will relapse."
- "I am afraid to tell you that I have declared bankruptcy and you will think I am not responsible."

The responses go on. There is one common, uniting element to this exercise. If done seriously and honestly, it is a tool of connectivity. It highlights that all of us, every single one, has had issues that have triggered shame. All of us, every single one, has failed in some fashion. All of us, every single one, has something we wish we could do over.

All of us, every single one, are human, fallible, and deserving of grace.

The place that grace must be extended first is to yourself. And then we have the absolute moral responsibility to extend it to one another. Hear me when I say that at some point in your life, you and everyone you know will desperately need it.

One compelling example of this same concept happened when I was working with a large division at a public university. I was encouraging the group to communicate more effectively. I challenged them to make a commitment to putting away their technology and pay complete attention to one another. It was going well for the first day. The second day, things changed.

During the evening between the training days, I had a personal crisis surface. I was across the country, thousands of miles away from my home, when my phone began to receive strings of text messages. They were from a family member who has battled mental health and drug addiction issues for years. They were threatening violence and I spent most of the night awake, alerting other family members and speaking with police about the situation. The text messages continued through the night and into the next day. I found myself standing at the podium with my cell phone face up, distracted every time it buzzed that a text was received.

I made a decision and turned to my audience. I said, "I realize that I am violating my own recommendation and getting distracted by my cell phone. I want to share with you something very personal to explain why. It is literally a safety issue for me and my family that I am monitoring."

I went on to share more about the family member's struggle with mental health and addiction and the history I had with this crippling issue.

By the end of the day, four people from different departments in the division had asked to speak privately to me. Each of them shared that they also were struggling either personally or with a close family member who was battling mental health and drug addiction issues. They each then went on to share their fear that someone else in the division would find out because each thought they were the only one there dealing with it.

The isolation that comes with believing you are the only one handling a crisis is real. The energy it takes to hide the truth is monumental. The worst part is, it is all based on a lie.

All of us, every single one, has experienced flashpoints that have affected us deeply. We are better together if we can share and build bridges in safe spaces with trusted allies.

Employers, take note! Do not pass on a job-seeker who has encountered a crisis. Especially in this day of social media and all the misinformation that is out in the Internet, do not pass on someone out of hand. I have seen people get completely buried in bad press for issues that later turned out to be unfounded and totally false. What really works? Look at credentials and then bring the person in to have a discussion face-to-face. Then decide.

I always encourage everyone to play offense. Do not bury the past when you are moving ahead. Be forthright about where you have been and what has happened along the way. This is in no way an endorsement for walking into a new opportunity and sharing negative impressions of former employers. Rather, it is an approach where you take the lead and share from your vantage point what occurred, and then being able to lay out your reasons why you know things went in a negative direction. All the work that you do to examine why things ended the way they did will inform your story. You also will be grounded in your truth and know that you now are pursuing opportunities from a wiser perspective. Tell your own story. Stand in your own truth. Demonstrate leadership under your own terms. Otherwise, you must know that new employers will have conducted extensive reviews into your past via social media and come to their own conclusions. It is your story. Play offense and explain it yourself.

I greatly admire Dr. Brene' Brown. Here are three quotes she offers that address this same subject:

- When we deny the story, it defines us. When we own the story, we can write a brave new ending.
- When we have the courage to walk into our story and own it, we get to write the ending.
- You either walk inside your story and own it, or you stand outside your story and hustle for your worthiness.

Avoid all self-handicapping behavior. Commit to doing the heavy lifting that needs to occur to be open, honest, transparent, and forthright. You will find that you will connect in meaningful ways with others who will hear your story, and resonate to events in their own lives that have been difficult to navigate. If they do not resonate with you, well, there is your answer. It likely is not a match with your value system and moral compass. Move on. There is no such thing as a once in a lifetime opportunity. The most important hurdle to clear is the one that lands you in the correct place as you move forward. Do not look the other way and ignore signals that are clear in order to get an offer. If you do, you will find yourself in a new role, standing at the same dead-end before long.

At the end of the day, what really works is what works for you. You are walking your unique journey. The key is to figure out how to surround yourself with supportive, honest people, and then develop a plan guided by purpose. There are waypoints all around you. Release yourself from shame and second-guessing, and whatever else is pulling you down, so you can follow them.

When we're growing up
There are all sorts of people telling us what to do
When really what we need is space
To work out who to be.
—Ellen Page

## Chapter 5

# TERROR, FREEFALL, AND BREAKING THROUGH

*"Ask and it will be given to you; search, and you will
find; knock and the door will be opened for you."*
—*Jesus*

At the end of the day, breaking through is more about embracing who you are than worrying about what others think. The hardest work just may be this particular step. Coming through storms in life will either take you farther off the track of self-discovery or allow you to come closer to understanding who you really are. Uniqueness is often labeled as something that is undesirable in this digital age. Do not fall into this trap. You can absolutely come through traumatic experiences with your moral compass intact, and stronger for having been in that space. It takes courage and faith in yourself. To quote Dr. Charles Stanley,

"You cannot be full of fear and full of faith at the same time."
Choose to let go of the fear.

Kintsugi is defined as, "golden joinery, or golden repair." It
is a Japanese art form also known as Kintsukuroi. When this
process is utilized, broken pottery is repaired with lacquer dusted
or mixed with powdered gold, silver, and platinum. Instead of
trying to disguise the damaged pieces of the broken pottery,
it treats the breakage as part of the history of the object. It is
something that is to be celebrated. The result is pottery that is
uniquely beautiful and stronger than the original.

That is what happens to us when we incorporate the broken-
ness into our history, and emerge stronger, more confident, and
uniquely beautiful. When the worst that can happen does, and
you conquer it, there is a strength that is added to the foundation.
It takes dragging the event out into the open, staring it down, and
determining how you want the breakthrough to happen. The ball
is in your court. Pick it up and start towards the goal.

So much of our self-view is driven by the self-talk in our own
heads. It is a process that we can and must control. Be purposeful
about what you allow to be taken in. One of my favorite poems,
by author Digby Wolfe, is a great message to play. It is entitled,
*Kids Who Are Different:*

Here's to kids who are different,
Kids who don't always get A's,
Kids who have ears
Twice the size of their peers,
And noses that go on for days.

Here's to the kids who are different,
Kids they call crazy or dumb,
Kids who don't fit,

With the guts and the grit,
Who dance to a different drum.

Here's to the kids who are different,
Kids with a mischievous streak,
For when they have grown,
As history has shown,
It's their difference that makes them unique.

Breaking through requires that you embrace and celebrate your uniqueness. We enter the world without all the trappings of self-doubt. What happens between that day and the day you find yourself in freefall, in a state of terror?

It likely is what you have always feared as the worst thing that can ever happen to you, happens.

Earlier I shared that journaling and working through the plans you will need to develop if the worst thing does, in fact, happen is very empowering. It keeps you on the pathway of playing offense. Having a knowledge base to pull from will give you a semblance of security. When you have your affairs in order, such as knowing your financial bottom line and resources to draw from it, gives you a thought-out starting point. You will be that much farther ahead when the freefall occurs. It will occur at some point in your life. Count on it.

One thing I discovered when I was going through my own freefall was somewhat shocking. In fact, I thought perhaps I was going a little bit crazy. I found myself in the midst of a transitional year in my career, as well as finding my way through a very painful divorce. I made the decision to move out of the place I loved and had called home for twenty years, into a new space to begin again.

In the mornings, I always tend to follow my routine, and part of that is making my bed each day. I lived quite close to the place where I worked. On those mornings when I was running late, I would skip making the bed. I found myself consumed with thoughts of the unmade bed all morning. They disrupted my day so badly that I began to skip lunch on those days and drive back to my new space, make my bed, and then return to work.

In short, I thought I was losing it.

I spoke to a counselor about what was happening. I was surprised at her assessment. She told me that often, when we find ourselves in freefall, we search for anything we can do to control what is happening around us. I was unable to control the fact that the bottom had dropped out of my marriage. One thing I could control each day? Whether or not my bed was made. She explained that bringing order to what I could control was helpful and organizing in a world that seemed quite chaotic.

Once I understood what was triggering my thoughts and behaviors, I began to harness that energy. I also decided to extend grace to myself. I decided to give myself a break.

The terror that accompanies the unknown is real. The trauma that happens as a result needs to be acknowledged and dealt with.

Trauma happens to everyone. The human experience is to know every emotion and one of the most powerful is the fear and terror that is inflicted by trauma. There are some who believe that our very entrance into the world, through our physical birth, is the first traumatic experience that we have imprinted on our psyche. When trauma is not addressed, it is a catalyst for shaping our behaviors. It can be a trigger for mental health issues. Trauma can, if allowed, handicap us in ways that prohibit us from rising to our full human potential. Breaking through the cycle requires not only an awareness of the role that trauma plays in our lives, but the ability to move through it in systematic, proven ways.

I have been very grateful for the University of Buffalo's School of Social Work's contribution in this arena. They have created, *The Institute on Trauma and Trauma-Informed Care (ITTIC)*. They offer data-driven approaches to handling trauma in the workplace. It includes providing their work, "Trauma-Informed Organizational Change Manual" to anyone who requests it. This is valuable whether you are an employee or an employer. The goal for the employee is to seek organizations who are thought-leaders, willing to invest in a positive work environment. The goal of the organization ought to be to provide such an environment.

Trauma-informed care is the approach of moving through life, especially the difficult chapters, understanding that trauma has shaped who we are. The adverse experiences begin in childhood and mold the adults that we become. Many are familiar with the term post-traumatic stress disorder (PTSD). We associate it with people who have been through unimaginable experiences in times of war, or after witnessing a horrific event. PTSD can certainly manifest itself after events like these. It can also surface after multiple small traumas are left unchecked and begin to layer one upon the other until cracks begin to surface.

One area that is less well-known regarding trauma is the phenomenon known as Secondary Traumatic Stress (STS). This is when symptoms of trauma occur to a person when they witness someone else being harmed. A good example of this is when we witness violence on the news and empathize with the person who is being harmed. With the increase in real-time coverage of events world-wide, STS is more prevalent than before. Vicarious Trauma (VT) occurs as a result of changing your world view in a negative fashion over time as you watch others facing adversity and hardship.

If trauma is not taken into consideration, it is very likely that re-traumatization will be the result. Consider the example of losing your job, and then not doing the work required to move through the trauma that was caused as a result. You very well may find another job, but you likely will carry fear and worry with you as you embark on the new opportunity. That will leave less energy to focus on the new role. It can also impact your decision-making process about what new role is viable, versus a life raft that has been thrown in your direction. Do not make this mistake.

Employers there are many tools for establishing a Trauma-Informed Organizational Model. An overall approach requires a paradigm shift that changes the focus from "What is wrong with that person?" to "What has happened to that person?"

We never know when someone is experiencing trauma from terror or freefall. There seems to be two different ways that we experience trauma. One is the cumulative effect of trauma that has occurred to us throughout our lives. The second is when trauma is triggered by an event that is acute. When you are in a supportive environment, it is easier to get your needs met so you can navigate through the obstacle. Trauma-informed care involves understanding the whole person and extending grace by default. Instead of finding yourself in an environment where there is a lack of support, only gossip and finger-pointing, you will find yourself in a space where the first reaction is an extension of help. There are five guiding principles of a trauma-informed approach:

- Safety.
- Choice.
- Collaboration.
- Trustworthiness.
- Empowerment.

Each of these elements is essential. Safety is rooted in the psychologically safe spaces that were defined earlier. It is also inclusive of physical safety. If this element is missing, any progress that is made will be shallow and likely will not last. When you are in freefall, safety is one of the first things that you will need in order to move ahead.

Choice is very important. Seeking out future opportunities that give degrees of freedom to you as you navigate the organization, will allow you to define your rights as well as your responsibilities. Keeping the lines of communication open and providing transparency is key. Many in the new COVID-19 world order feel safer being allowed to continue to work from home. This is lessening the stress associated with the fear of the unknown as we continue to grapple with the novel virus.

Collaboration is one of the tenants of a trauma-informed approach for good reason. This environment allows workers to participate in creating their working environments versus having leadership dictate how things will be. This creates buy-in and a sense of control that is very crucial in creating an environment that is addressing trauma in positive ways.

Trustworthiness is a staple of a positive work environment that is less likely to re-traumatize employees. The most important part of trustworthiness is walking the walk. Follow-through is emphasized. It is better to not begin any sort of intervention than to begin work with employees and then put it on the shelf. To build trustworthiness, employees need to see that the organization is invested in their safety and well-being. This takes away the stress of worrying when the next shoe will drop. Transparency is so important. It is, of course, impossible to make all negative situations go away. For example, layoffs and downsizing occur in the business world. If employers are transparent about what is happening and present pathways forward to support their workforce, it will inspire faith in trustworthiness and loyalty to the organization overall.

Empowerment is one of the most essential tools you can access to work towards your own breakthrough. The loss of control over one's circumstances is both terrifying and completely disempowering. By seeking out people and organizations who are actively looking to put the locus of control back into your hands you will be a step closer to breaking the freefall. One of the factors is successfully navigating the issue at hand that is your "worst that can happen." Focusing on your strengths and reimagining how you can move ahead is time that is well spent. This is where investment in self-care and self-discovery will prove so powerful. Do not let up. Do not give up. Create solutions and work methodically towards them.

According to the ITTIC's holistic description of what happens to us, as a result of the impact of trauma and adversity, is explained in their literature. The ITTIC describes emotional regulation as being negatively affected and showing up as a loss of impulse control, difficulty interpreting emotional cues, loss of trust in the reliability of others, and establishing a predictable sense of self. Regarding cognitive functioning, trauma and adversity affects one's ability to form memories, learn and concentrate, make decisions and process and express language. The effect on physical and mental health can be demonstrated by developing diabetes, heart disease, cancer and other ailments, engaging in substance abuse, suicide attempts, and developing sexually transmitted diseases. Relationally you may also suffer as it becomes more difficult to identify and form healthy relationships, trust issues, the ability to express needs and wants to others, as well as set boundaries. Perceptions and beliefs become skewed as core beliefs about oneself, others and the world become blurred. The ability to experience hope can also be damaged.

Current data supports that more than 45 million Americans experience mental health issues. More than 80% of adults will deal with a mental illness event at some point in their lives. Some are triggered by events, such as job loss, and can resolve if they are treated. Many people struggle with lifelong mental illness issues, and something that compounds their lives like a job loss can serve as a catalyst to a more challenging state of mental health. There are many categories of mental illness. The following is a partial list:

- Mood disorders (such as depression or bipolar disorder).
- Anxiety disorders.
- Personality disorders.
- Psychotic disorders (such as schizophrenia).
- Eating disorders.
- Trauma-related disorders (such as post-traumatic stress disorder).
- Substance abuse disorders.

Trauma and mental health are intrinsically linked. By finding mechanisms to empowerment and hitting the reset button after you find yourself in freefall is something that absolutely has to occur. The tools that are available to take you through your time of introspection and self-care are organizing and must be completed. Finding the people who you can turn to that are willing to be honest, and vulnerable, and most importantly, truthful, will serve you well.

There are two ways to stymie your progress. One is not to take the first step and ask for the help you need. The second is to not follow through once you start down the path.

I know it is scary.

At the lowest point in my past, I found myself freefalling through a very dark valley. I was isolated and did not reach out for help. I found myself succumbing to very dark thoughts that eventually led me to a plan of action to solve everything.

The problem? It was the wrong plan of action.

Prior to that terrible week, I would have shared that my belief was that anyone who ever made the decision to take his or her own life was selfish. I would spout the often-heard mantra, "It is a permanent solution to a temporary problem." I thought I knew a lot more about it than I actually did.

The day I found myself standing in that space it seemed to be the only choice. THE ONLY CHOICE. I could not imagine moving forward. I was totally exhausted. I did not have the support system built around me that I needed, and I felt shame, which inhibited my ability to be vulnerable and reach out for help. I lost sight of the fact that there were people out in the world who did care for me and would help me if they had any idea of my intentions.

I did not activate my network during my season of freefall. Instead, I spent my time working my plan to overdose on a cocktail of painkillers from a recent surgery. Then I wrote letters of apology and followed my plan.

As the universe would have it, God showed up. A series of events that can only be described as a miracle sent a friend to my front door to nearly break it down. She would later share that as she sat at her office in a meeting, she felt an overwhelming sense of dread and a directive to come to my home. She listened, and because she did, I am here today to share the experience.

I made it through my freefall due to what I solidly believe is divine intervention. Whatever your higher power is, whatever you reach into yourself and beyond for help, make space in your day to connect to it. Whenever things look as bleak as you have ever known, remember that some days all you have to do is simply show up and know that there are greater plans for you. Freefall is scary. Freefall is traumatic. Freefall is also your opportunity to be able to make the biggest breakthrough that you have ever experienced.

One phenomenon that I have witnessed is that freefall is compounded when the loss of a job is surrounded by negative work circumstances. When someone is released from an organization that is corrupt, or laced with leadership that do not display values, the bigger the betrayal seems to be. I heard someone exclaim once, "That is the worst place I have ever worked for, and STILL they do not want me!"

Count your blessings. Do not confuse your sense of self and what you are worth with the judgement of a company, especially one that is exhibiting no ethical leadership. Your value to the universe is not predicated on any place of employment, especially one that is morally bankrupt. Remember when you find yourself in freefall that your skill sets and abilities did not vanish when you changed positions. Your sum total is so much greater than any position you will ever hold.

Remember to embrace who you are. You are the architect of your life. Go get it. Do not forget to look up. The daybreak is coming.

# SETTING YOUR RULES

*"Anyone who ever gave you confidence, you owe them a lot."*
—*Truman Capote*

It takes time, effort, and bravery to set your own rules. Many times, the socialization that happens throughout our upbringing sends us the wrong messages. We fall into traps that tell us that we do not want to stand out. That we are to be seen and not heard. That it is rude to ask for what you want and need.

I have come to believe that the answer to this struggle was written long ago, and has come to be known as, The Golden Rule:

"Therefore, whatever you desire for men to do to you, you shall also do to them; for this is the law and the prophets." Matthew 7:12.

Sometimes, even if this is your practice, you may still find yourself struggling with setting boundaries and communicating expectations to others. It is an easy rabbit hole in which to fall.

There are many people, Dr. Phil McGraw included, who frequently state that you teach people how to treat you. By tolerating bad behavior, you reinforce someone else's right to treat you in a way that violates your rules and moral compass.

I am not referring to a single event. As we all navigate through our days, we will encounter negative occurrences with others. These require us to slow down, take a breath, and decide if it is likely to occur again, and require attention, or to turn the other cheek and move on. What needs our attention is the ongoing negative treatment that we accept from others that is demoralizing and draining.

One of the statements I often hear when people refer to someone who is rude, abrasive, or worse is an excuse. It usually sounds something like this:

"That is just how (fill in the name) is!"

My response? "No. That is how you allow (fill in the name) to act."

It is useful to establish guiding principles when you begin to have these important interactions. Coming from the position of extending grace, a major one is to assume that everyone is acting with the best of intentions, and to the best of their ability. Secondly, ask that you speak directly and candidly, especially when there is a difference of opinion. Always encourage spirited debate, never allowing the conversation to go negative in any personal fashion. Lastly, when a difference of opinion occurs, especially in group settings or meetings, speak directly to the person with whom you differ. Do not allow yourself to get pulled into sidebar conversations about others, so you model the principle you want to have extended to you.

Crucial conversations will be successful if you invest time in figuring out what factors are contributing to ineffective communication. It takes a lot of effort to be an active listener, mindful of the exchange. It is totally worth it. Setting up an environment where you can devote your undivided attention to the crucial conversation is a proven strategy for success. Put your technology away. Check your body language. Is it inviting? Or does it send an invisible "Beware of the Dog!" message? Following up in writing is also organizing and clarifying for both parties.

Resist the urge to talk just to avoid silence. It takes practice to get used to the silence. Do the work involved. The more comfortable you can get in your skin, allowing yourself the ability to process and think versus constantly talking, the better your communication skills will become.

As you set rules, be sure you consider what generation you fall into, and what that generational mindset brings with it. Your generation is defined by common experiences and shared values and can vary widely from others who fall in different generations. A generation is a society-wide peer group, born over approximately twenty years who possess common characteristics, distinct attitudes, behaviors, expectations and motivational buttons. By understanding generational differences, you will set yourself up to be able to understand the role it plays as you work towards effective communication.

The XYZ Strategy is one tool you can employ to stay abreast of generational differences. X stands for X-out stereotypes. Do not fall into the trap of making sweeping generalizations about any group, including generational categories. Actively work to understand the factors that defines the generational categories. It is easy to understand, for example, the role that technology has played in defining younger generations as compared to their more senior counterparts. Y stands for Y-know your story, what is your style? What is your motivation? How do you communicate? Handle conflict? What areas do you need to improve? Finally, Z stands for Z-zealous. Zealously advocate for yourself. Zealously work to understand the stories of others and how they affect their style of interacting.

When you go about the work of setting your rules, one of the first must be that you learn how to set healthy boundaries and to not allow anyone to treat you badly. You can do this by paying close attention to the way you respond to how you are treated. Your response will either reinforce the negative behavior or decrease it if it happens a second time.

Once a negative pattern of interacting with someone occurs, it becomes far more difficult to correct the course of action. The longer the bad behavior has been allowed to continue, the longer it will take to undo it. It is far better to invest time up front and course correct right away.

One of the best ways you can turn the tide towards a more positive direction is to allow the people you interact with some wiggle room. When someone says something rude to you, for example, extend some grace, but also hold him or her accountable. Do it in a respectful tone and do it in a manner where it is just the two of you. Publicly shaming someone will not get you the result you are seeking. You can phrase it along these lines:

"I am hoping you do not realize this, but I wanted to share that when you undercut my idea in the staff meeting, it left me with nowhere to move all the work I have been doing forward with the group. How can we get to a better place?"

We do not know what is happening with someone on any given day, so extending grace is always the goal. You just need to be certain that in doing so you are also taking care of yourself and creating an environment that is positive so you can thrive. Lead by example. And on those days when you fall short, take the initiative to make things right. Extending grace to yourself is something that always needs to occur.

Retaliation is never the answer.

Leading by example is powerful. So is consistency in your approach to setting your own rules. Reinforce the behavior you want extended to you by responding in positive ways. Another tool to use is questioning the person who is not meeting your standards. For example, with a colleague who constantly is cancelling meetings at the last minute, making your calendar impossible to manage, you might probe this way: "How are things going for you? Are our meeting times not convenient on your schedule, because we can move them. I am sure you do not know, but it has caused me some challenges due to the lost time since we seem to continue to cancel them week-to-week. Thoughts?"

Many times, simply opening the door with the conversation helps to open people's eyes to what their behavior is costing you. This can then help you to be very transparent and establish boundaries that are clear, as well as reasonable for both of you.

Several years ago, I accepted a position in a very rural, southern part of the country. As I was being introduced to the organization for one of my first public speaking engagements I was forced, on the spot, to make a decision about setting my expectations for how I would be treated. The gentleman who was introducing me was a vice president. As he called me to the podium he was joking and laughing with the audience. He was well known and had been a member of the community for many years. He knew I was raised in Kentucky and decided to say the following to me as I was ascending the stairs to the take the microphone:

"Hey folks, let's welcome Kimberly. She is the newest member of the team here. We want to make her feel right at home even though she is a Northern sympathizer. I guess we can forgive her for that, though, because she's easy on the eyes!"

My heart began to race. I literally could not believe what I was hearing. I was also painfully aware that as a new member of the team, I was a virtual unknown and did not have any political capital to spend with the crowd. The man who had introduced me was smiling ear-to-ear, fully believing he had just paid me a wonderful compliment.

I stumbled through my remarks. Later I asked to speak to the man in private. I had taken time to organize my thoughts and was able to talk without getting emotional. I explained to him that what had happened was deeply offensive to me. I found no humor in jokes about the division in our country that had catapulted us into a civil war. I also did not want to be introduced with a reference to my physical appearance. I made it clear that I expected to be introduced with my professional accomplishments highlighted. That what had happened could never, ever happen again. I also followed my own advice by beginning with the acknowledgement that he likely had no idea why this had affected me the way it did. It allowed him to hear me. Truly hear me. It affected a change that was positive.

Do not reinforce behavior that is not desirable. Again, it may seem like it is easier in the short run to give someone a pass, but in fact exactly the opposite is true. Once you have come through your journey of self-discovery and are embarking on a new direction it is very important that you communicate how you expect to be treated. This is especially true as you enter a new role. Above all, you want to control setting your rules versus being reactionary.

As you work through this process, remember that you will encounter bad people. Extending grace is a tenant I live by. It has gotten me into exactly the sort of trouble I am describing, though, as I continued to extend grace to people who were not my supporters.

One of my favorite Maya Angelou's quotes? "When someone shows you who they are, believe them the first time."

Trust your instincts. Then act. When you are setting your rules, you are the architect. Take the wisdom from the lessons that have been learned and put them to use.

At times, you may find that you are labeled as a troublemaker. A rabble-rouser. That is okay. As long as you are clear in your value system, and extending grace, you also should give yourself permission to put your hand up. One of the best pieces of advice I have heard is that you do not have to give long explanations about your boundaries. Or any explanation at all. Sometimes it is just as effective to say, "That does not work for me." There is no need to be disrespectful when you stand your ground. Just be sure to stand in your truth. When you have something to say, say it. Truth has a funny way of finding its way to the light.

Several years ago, I received an SOS call from a colleague. She had taken a position working as an accountant with a company that utilized her throughout the tax season. From the outset, she was not treated respectfully by the head of the firm. She was reluctant to speak up, worried that rocking the boat would cost her the new position. So, she acquiesced and sat silent at meetings and literally pretended not to hear remarks that were undercutting of her and her work.

The head of the firm set the tone for the organization. The negative culture that resulted was very stressful in which to work. Days were agonizing. Perhaps the worst day of the week was Sunday as she prepared to face the week ahead.

The hours grew longer as Tax Day approached. Then she began working through the weekends to meet the demands. She produced excellent results for the firm but continued to spiral in her ability to set any boundaries for how she was treated. Her reward for getting the firm and all their clients through the tax season successfully?

She was abruptly called into the boss's office under the guise of projecting the next year's forecasts. Instead of finding herself in a discussion about forecasting, she was fired immediately.

When people show you who they are, believe them the first time.

Once she shed the negative work environment, she found that her skill sets quickly landed her employment elsewhere. The lesson learned was that putting up with being treated badly does not guarantee you will retain your job, no matter how skilled you are.

Another lesson has been a theme that has been overarching throughout this entire writing. You are you. You are not your job. Do not confuse the two. Do not compromise your boundaries to hang onto a position if you are being treated badly.

Another example where people find trouble establishing boundaries is when they are approached while working successfully at an organization and offered a change. The change may, from the outset, look terrific. To everyone except the employee who receives the offer. It may be a promotion. It may be a relocation to a great geographical location. It may be added responsibilities.

The problem occurs if the employee does not take the time to conduct a thorough inventory of their personal goals and responsibilities to see if it makes sense to accept the offer. It is always advisable to ask for time to think things through even if at first pass it appears like exactly the offer you have been dreaming of all of your life. Time is your friend. Use it.

The next step is to do a truly deep dive into what the change means for you. There is no perfect scenario. There is also no such thing as a once in a lifetime opportunity. They tend to cycle around again if you decide this is not the time to take that leap. Be honest with yourself.

If you know your tendencies, and where your strengths and weaknesses lie, it will help you to discern what the best answer is. It is also very important that you do not cave into pressure, worried you might disappoint a boss or colleague. Figure out your work/life balance, then make your decision. Thoughtfully and deliberately. Then schedule the meeting to let the organization know what that decision is. Thank them for the opportunity and then accept it or explain why it does not work for you at that particular time. Hold your boundary line firm. At the end of the day, you are the one who will live with the decision. If the outcome is not positive, it will also spill over and affect those in your circle who care for you.

Consider this excerpt. It speaks to the heart of breaking out of old patterns and setting your rules and boundaries:

### Chapter 1
I walk down the street.
There is a deep hole in the sidewalk.
I fall in. I am lost... I am hopeless.
It isn't my fault.
It takes forever to find a way out.

### Chapter 2
I walk down the same street.
There is a deep hole in the sidewalk.
I pretend I don't see it. I fall in again.
I can't believe I am in this same place.
But it isn't my fault.
It still takes a long time to get out.

## Chapter 3
I walk down the same street.
There is a deep hole in the sidewalk.
I see it there.
I still fall in… it's a habit… but, my eyes are open.
I know where I am.
It is my fault.
I get out immediately.

## Chapter 4
I walk down the same street.
There is a deep hole in the sidewalk.
I walk around it.

## Chapter 5
I walk down another street.

—Portia Nelson

This excerpt speaks to several key issues. Foundational is accountability. Accountability to yourself first. Once you achieve that goal, you can then seek to be accountable to others. Recognizing what is happening, taking responsibility for it, and then adjusting your behavior is critical if you are going to set rules that work.

Beyond teaching people how to treat you, it is imperative that you learn how to treat yourself. Setting rules for what you are allowed to say and do to yourself, is something many people never consider. Maintaining a physically healthy state is vitally important. Equally important is maintaining a healthy psyche and spirit. Check in with yourself regularly. Are you treating yourself as well as you treat others? If not, why not? Isolate any behaviors that are violating the rules you set for yourself and how you are treated. Then, systematically address them one-by-one until they are permanently eliminated.

Setting rules, whether for yourself or others, must consider diversity, and the unique pathways each of us have come down. If we are going to be successful at setting rules and boundaries that are both reasonable and achievable, we must be purposeful in seeking to understand one another. This is not a passive effort. It takes work, and a sense of purpose.

It is our responsibility to educate ourselves so that we are culturally competent. By definition, cultural competency is an awareness of, respect for, and attention to the diversity of the people and community in which we interact. Our attitudes should reflect that awareness and an appreciation for difference. Diversity is defined differently. A great working definition is, a quality or state of having many different forms, types, ideas, processes and methods. Diversity is achieved when the organizations we interact with are a true reflection of our communities.

Inclusion involves a clear recognition that people are sometimes treated unfairly or excluded because of their differences. We must be proactive in removing barriers and engage all groups.

We are never going to be totally successful at setting rules for ourselves and others until every voice is recognized and valued.

Chimamanda Ngozi Adichie has contributed a wonderful narrative by way of a TED Talk in 2009. It is entitled, "The Danger of a Single Story." She shares her views on how we do a disservice to anyone if we define him or her through a single lens, or a single story. As we grapple with the search for a deeper understanding of one another, we must be very cautious not to fall into a trap by defining anyone on their appearance, country of origin, religious beliefs, sexual orientation, or any other factor. I cannot say this with enough conviction. At the heart of setting your rules is adherence to respect for yourself and others. This cannot occur absent understanding and celebrating differences.

Take some time to inventory the rules that mean the most to you. They should dovetail with your value system. They will compliment your line in the sand. List them out and revisit them often. Rank order them to reflect their importance to you. As you check in, always ask yourself if they are currently reflective of where you stand on this issue. Are they accurate? How do you know?

Embrace truth telling and honesty. Begin by modeling that behavior for yourself. Setting your rules and following them benefits everyone. You become a positive force in the universe.

## Chapter 7

# KICKING THE IMPOSTER OUT

———— ⚡ ————

*"Believe you can and you're halfway there."*
—*Theodore Roosevelt*

Once you have completed the necessary work to discover where your moral compass lies, what your non-negotiable, drop-dead line in the sand is, and understand what drives you from your most personal depths, there is another obstacle to overcome. This particular obstacle is crippling. Perhaps even more so than any other.

Once you have your house in order, and know where you stand, who will support you, and how to stop the negative narrative that runs through your head, another monster will invariably pop out from under the bed.

It has a proper title that is backed up with longitudinal research. I am referring to: The Imposter Syndrome.

The Imposter Syndrome is unique. It is not to be confused with being placed into a position that you are totally unprepared to assume. It is not to be confused with lack of preparation, education, or work ethic.

It is a syndrome that almost everyone experiences at some point. A proper definition is that it is a complete collection of feelings that you are inadequate no matter what evidence exists that contradicts them. It is persistent, destructive, and can be hard to overcome unless you stand up and punch that monster squarely in the nose.

Earlier I challenged you to identify the source of the negative voices playing on the soundtrack in your head and to, one-by-one, eliminate them. Pull that tool out of your toolkit when addressing this monster as well. That soundtrack is gasoline on the fire of The Imposter Syndrome.

Conversely, remember to access your support system. Who is your squad? Who are the people in your circle that I have termed your "SOS" folks? By that I mean, who can you text SOS to at any time of the day or night and they know to stop what they are doing to come to your aid? This should be a very small, very tight group who you can be certain are loyal.

Identifying the syndrome takes bravery. It takes a lot of vulnerability. The great news is that by being vulnerable, you set the tone for others to follow your lead. The research tells us that everyone has struggled with this syndrome at some point in his or her journey. A good leader will share their experience, and thereby extend grace to their employees to be transparent as well. Shine a light on the syndrome, and the commonalities that everyone has with respect to it. This will begin the process of overcoming it altogether.

There are always opportunities for everyone to grow and develop. If you are completely confident in everything you are doing in your professional life, you likely have outgrown your role. Stretching and challenging yourself in new and meaningful ways is healthy. Giving into a syndrome that is trying to convince you that you are not supposed to be where you are is not.

A very common theme that plays out in The Imposter Syndrome is an overwhelming feeling that you do not belong. You are somehow other-than. Feelings of inadequacy creep into your thought processes. Even when there is apparent, demonstrable success, the negative soundtrack continues to play, and you begin to believe you are creating a façade, rather than value added. The voice grows louder and louder, often screaming, "What if everyone finds out that I am NOT supposed to be here?"

Once the cycle begins, it can become very insidious. Repeatedly I have watched clients spend more time being frightened by the syndrome, and worse yet, doing things that feed the beast.

I once worked with a young executive who was elevated to the leadership team in a public university. He shared with me that he was putting his phone in his lap at the leadership team meetings and texting a colleague his point of view before actually offering it to the president. He thought he could trust this colleague. He was coming from a place of fear. He thought he was ensuring that he would not make a misstep. What he did was exactly the opposite.

The colleague ended up sharing what was happening in the meetings with the president, who then took a long pause to examine his decision to elevate the new member of the team in the first place. That is when I became involved and began to walk through the journey to understand what was driving the feelings of inadequacy. It was clearly not from the inability to do the work or add value. It stemmed directly from feeling as if he was not good enough to be in that seat.

Those negative feelings were spilling over into behaviors that were reinforcing his fear and drawing others into the circle. He was also making another big mistake: he was a very humble man, and a gentle spirit. He was a contrast of sorts with others at the table who were hard-wired to be hard charging. The president had made a wise decision by adding him to the team, but the opportunity for success was slipping away.

When the new executive was asked his opinion outright, he would drop his eyes, let his shoulders slump, and answer in very quiet tones. Worse yet? He began each response reminding everyone on the team that he was the new person on the block. "Well, I realize I am brand new so this might not be the best idea, but…" Just like that, he framed every contribution in a way that essentially served as a boat anchor. No matter how brilliant his answer was, it was set up to fail from the start by reminding everyone that he was uncomfortable in his own skin. How then, could anything he offered be valuable? His fear of being an imposter was fueling his behaviors and responses, leading everyone on the team to the wrong point of view: the one he held that he did not belong there.

This scenario ended successfully for the new executive. It did take work for him to sort through what was happening inside of him that was showing up in the workplace. Once that turned a positive corner, he was then able to draw attention to the things he needed to demonstrate, which was talent, drive and commitment to the team. He was value-added, not an imposter in the role.

One of the biggest hurdles to clear in the battle with The Imposter Syndrome is the feeling of dread that everyone is going to find out that you are not supposed to be there. I encourage clients to make a list of the worst outcomes that they can imagine. We then sit with that list, and take a rational, eyes wide-open approach to dealing with each item. Sometimes, items feel a lot less scary once they are written down. It is unlikely that many of them will ever come to fruition. If they do, having a plan in place to deal with them is enormously empowering. One thing I know from personal experience is that once something from that list occurs, and you make it to the other side safely, you will never be as frightened of it ever again.

The Imposter Syndrome can also be fed with thoughts of not earning your way, but by just being lucky. That your appointment was a fluke. That given the chance, your boss would choose someone else for the role.

Luck is not a bad thing. Having connections and being in the right place at the right time are fortuitous. Just guard against mistaking the role that luck, or a God Wink, that puts you in the right place at the right time with the notion that you do not belong.

Being astute and understanding the culture of your organization will go a long way in overcoming feelings of inadequacy or setting yourself up to fail. When I was in the last stages of my doctoral work, I found myself constructing my dissertation plan. I was a full-time worker, with a houseful of young children, also working full time on my doctoral work.

I met with my committee and finally was able to come to a consensus on what I could research. It was in the springtime, and I went on my way to complete this last step. I attacked it with fierceness, able to see the end of the line just ahead of me. I put myself on a strict writing schedule, and showed back up on campus, happily handing my typewritten dissertation to my committee chair. I will never forget what she said next.

She told me that I could not turn it in after just six months' work. When I asked why, she shared with me that she knew from experience that my committee members would not think it was good enough. When I asked how that could be possible, since neither she nor they had read it yet, she responded, "Kimberly, no one will think you have produced a product worthy of receiving your degree in just six months. You simply have not had enough time to ripen on the vine yet."

In this instance, I found myself having The Imposter Syndrome thrust upon me. Instead of looking at what I did, culture was dictating if I were worthy of entering the club of professionals with a doctorate. I went home, put my dissertation into my desk drawer, and returned six months later. I submitted the exact same document to my committee. I went through the process without incident and was granted my degree.

Understand that overcoming The Imposter Syndrome is multi-faceted. You must believe in yourself, encourage others to believe in you, and be smart politically. Listen to the messages you receive. Which ones are real? Which ones are lies? Which ones can be handled, and which ones are culturally set in stone?

The idea that you have fooled everyone, and do not belong can be reinforced by downplaying success. When praise comes your direction, it is very important that you are comfortable accepting it.

I believe it is vital to always award credit where it is due, especially to your team and support personnel. What is detrimental is when there is an absolute feeling of being uncomfortable simply saying, "Thank you," when a compliment comes your way. So many people have integrated The Imposter Syndrome so deeply, they are painfully uncomfortable accepting any accolades. As soon as a compliment comes in, you can almost hear an audible whoosh as they bat it across the net back at the person who delivered it. I hear statements such as:

"It was not really me. The credit goes to my team."

Or, "I appreciate that, but it was not that hard to begin with. It is not a big deal."

This can make the person delivering the praise feel uncomfortable or even silly, but there is a far darker ramification. It sows the seeds that you do not belong or cannot perform without significant shoring up from others.

It takes practice, but you can learn to sit in that space and be comfortable with praise. Get comfortable with silent pauses. Do not give in to the urge to fill up those pauses with chatter. Two simple words get the job done: "Thank you."

On the journey to kicking the imposter out of your life, journaling is a mighty weapon. It is important to recognize the triggers that activate the monster. Journaling will reveal patterns. Is it a particular person that starts the dominos to fall? Is it a meeting that you are required to attend? Once you know what the triggers are, you can set about to eliminate them.

It is important to always remember that no matter what your perceptions are, no one can know everything. No one. Those who attempt to perpetuate that they have all the answers are demonstrating their own insecurities. It is a fallacy to look at someone else and believe they do not need help. We all do. The greatest leaders are transparent about the areas where they need help. This then allows their teams to follow suit. It is a great sign of strength to ask for help. It is also empowering, and freeing. Leadership is both about mastering the content of your field, as well as understanding where to go for assistance.

Consider a highly functioning president and board of directors. The very best example of the strength of this relationship can be seen at their meetings. The strongest presidents will have their executive teams accompany them to these meetings. It encourages transparency. More importantly, it demonstrates that the leader understands that no one has all the answers. For example, when asked about the budget, the president can answer, but certainly not in the level of detail that the chief financial officer can. By turning that question over to the CFO, the president is modeling by example what their job actually is. The president's job is to put capable people in the top roles and then stepping aside so they can perform those roles.

By acknowledging that no one can know everything, leaders dispel the myth of perfectionism. It is not sustainable to try to be perfect. Messing up is part of life. How you handle the fallout of messing up is the most important aspect.

It is natural for employees to model the behavior that is set by the leadership. If the leadership is modeling a pattern of perfectionism, employees will strive to do the same. This will ultimately reinforce The Imposter Syndrome. Perfectionism is not attainable and not sustainable. It will grind workers into the ground as they attempt to achieve it. It also will falsely perpetuate the notion that one is not good enough because they know they cannot achieve perfection.

Remember the executive who was taking endless PowerPoint notes in order to field every question that could possibly be asked during her presentation? Not being comfortable in her space was driving her fear of ever saying, "I do not know." Not knowing does not negate your ability to be successful. It simply exercises the muscle of figuring out who to go to in order to obtain the information you are missing. The feelings of inadequacy are hallmarks of The Imposter Syndrome. The root of the problem is that often those feelings are lies. Lies that we tell ourselves. Know this: feeling inadequate does not mean that you are.

What if the worst happens? What if you find yourself right in the middle of a great big failure? It is inevitable that somewhere along the way, failure will occur. Failure in your professional life. Failure in your personal life. Do not allow The Imposter Syndrome to compound the difficulties that come along during these times.

Again, journaling is your friend. Problem solving your way out of failure can be a great learning and growing experience. Not allowing yourself to be paralyzed by failure is key. Remember Lieutenant Dan? It was a long way back from the devastating injury that altered the course of his life. At the end, he was glad to be alive, and thankful for the future that was ahead of him. I realize this is a movie, but I can attest to this personally. Failure can be a launching pad to a new place in your life that is more satisfying and beyond all of your biggest dreams and plans. You simply must believe in yourself, and your ability to rebound. Defeat simply cannot be an option.

Making mistakes is a big part of life. How you handle mistakes that you make, or mistakes made by those around you, is very important. Extend grace. Be forthright and transparent. Lead by example: "I am sorry." "I am responsible." "How can I help?" Garner support from others as you work your way out of the aftermath of a mistake.

Just as perfectionism is non-existent, so is the idea of perfect people. Making a mistake does not mean you do not belong in your role. It means you are human. Forgive yourself and others. Forgiveness is one of the most powerful gifts you possess.

Embracing your excellence is a powerful way to combat The Imposter Syndrome. Stop accepting the lies that you are not enough. Start accepting praise when it is offered. Get comfortable in your own skin. We all are fearfully and wonderfully made. Every one of us has intrinsic worth and value and gifts that are uniquely ours to offer to this world. Kick the imposter out and embrace the person you are.

## Chapter 8

# MASTERING THE ART OF NEGOTIATION

*"Everything you've ever wanted is on the other side of fear"*
—*George Addair*

You have come through the firestorm. You have taken the time to do the hard work of finding your core value system and where your moral compass truly lies. You have received a new opportunity and completed what is necessary to shake The Imposter Syndrome. You know you belong and are ready to step up to the plate.

What is next?

One of the most important steps to complete the journey is mastering the art of negotiation. So many people are exquisitely uncomfortable with this process and subsequently handicap themselves before they ever sit down in their new office.

One of the roots that run deep, and lead to this misstep is a deep-seated feeling of not being worthy. The flames of that fire can be fed in many negative ways. When you take a hard look at where it begins, it usually leads to messages that were received way back in childhood.

The expectation of adults around us, as we develop, is easily assimilated in a belief system that can become part of our psyche in ways in which we may not be aware. It is very important to raise awareness about these internal messages and deliberately redirect them in a positive direction.

There was a very interesting study that was conducted by Professors Robert Rosenthal and Lenore Jacobson. They titled it, "The Harvard Test of Inflected Acquisition (Harvard TIA)." The test consisted of accessing school-aged children. Working directly with the teachers of these children, the professors asked if they could administer two tests to the groups. The first test was going to identify those students who displayed high ability. They labeled these students, "spurters." The second test was administered at a future date to assess whether they had, in fact, successfully identified gifted students.

The results from the second test did indeed reveal that the spurters gained 50% higher scores than their counterparts from the time of the original assessment. There was one problem. It was a big one.

At the end of the second assessment, the professors revealed that they were actually conducting a social experiment. They had randomly assigned the children into two groups and labeled one group the spurters. They then shared with the teachers who was in that bogus high ability group. What happened next was astonishing.

The teachers' expectations of the spurters was determined to be the singular difference in the markedly improved scores.

Simply put, they expected those students to do better, and as a result, they did.

Oftentimes it is thoroughly unintentional when adults plant seeds that influence the development of a young person's sense of accomplishment and self-worth. It is incumbent upon each of us to examine our personal feelings and determine, as adults, which are valid, and which are running a false narrative that impedes our progress forward. To quote Laozi, "If you do not change direction, you may end up where you are heading."

Throughout my life, I often heard my mother say, "Children will live up to, or down to, whatever is expected of them."

Religion can be another powerful tool that can have an unintended negative impact. In the King James version of the Bible, there is a very popular, often quoted verse from the book of Proverbs. "Pride goeth before destruction, and haughty spirit before a fall. —Proverbs, 16:18."

Do not misunderstand my message. I am not condoning haughtiness or arrogance. I am advocating for understanding your true value as you begin negotiating your package deal from a new opportunity free from false baggage hanging around from the past.

There is a body of research that also demonstrates that women fail far more profoundly at negotiating than their male counterparts. The discrepancy in pay between the genders continues to be an issue to resolve. In fact, each year, fluctuating a bit in April, "Equal Pay Day" occurs. This is the symbolic date that highlights the gender pay gap. It is the day that a female must work to earn the same salary that her male counterpart earns by the last day of the prior year.

If you factor in the data that proves that women fail to negotiate an equitable starting rate of pay, you can see how the ability to draw a fair salary is compounded. Women often start behind the eight ball and then are negatively impacted by gender inequities in the workplace, especially regarding pay. Longitudinal data has demonstrated that a woman who routinely negotiates salary and subsequent increases will earn over one million more dollars by the time she retires than one who does not.

One of the realities of living in the 21st century is the fact that many working adults are living in what has come to be called, "the Sandwich Generation." Financial pressures are exerted from two directions. Many people are raising children, and also caring for elderly friends and family members. People are living longer on average. Many are struggling with health issues that require a great deal of support. The financial challenges to meet the demands from all sides can be overwhelming. This is yet another reason to be certain that you negotiate effectively to maximize the dollar amount that you earn.

Returning to gender inequities, it should be noted that Lenore J. Weitzman shared sobering data in her book entitled, "The Divorce Revolution: The Unexpected Social and Economic Consequences for Women and Children in America." Regarding divorce, Weitzman reports that a woman's standard of living falls by 73% on average after a divorce while men's rises by 42% on average.

Weitzman is not alone in her journey to raise the awareness of the inequities faced by women while navigating the negotiating process in the workplace. Linda Babcock and Sara Laschever have published extensively on this topic. One of their seminal works is entitled, *"Women Don't Ask."*

As I have studied this phenomenon, I often frame it for audiences by referring to Dorothy from, *"The Wizard of Oz."* Think about it. Dorothy comes from the mid-West and is socialized early in the movie to be quiet and stay out of everyone's way. She is a pleaser. As she is journeying along the Yellow Brick

Road, she picks up everyone she encounters along the way and offers to help them solve their problems. It is gracious, with the exception that she propels her problem to the end of an ever-growing line. By the time she finally addresses her issue and is standing in the basket of the hot air balloon with the Wizard, she again sandbags her ability to get what she needs for herself. Do you remember why? She jumps out of the basket because her dog, Toto, has gotten free from her embrace and ran away. Dorothy catches her dog only to turn around and watch helplessly as the Wizard ascends in the hot air balloon eliminating what she believed to be all her options to return home.

I realize that this is a reference to a movie, and not a real-life situation, but there are lessons to be learned here. In her efforts to be gracious and helpful, Dorothy neglected to extend those same sentiments to herself. The other lesson to be learned is a powerful one. When I stand before audiences and ask what was said when Glenda the Good Witch floats down to Oz to talk with Dorothy, people invariably say, "Click your heels together three times." While that is correct, the discussion before that began with Dorothy asking Glenda why she had not shared that she had the power all along to get herself back to Kansas.

The simple, empowering answer? "You had to learn it for yourself."

Negotiating can be intimidating, but each of us has the power to stand up and do what is necessary to be treated fairly. Accepting less than you are worth will send the signal that you are less valuable than your colleagues. It also signals the same message to future employers. The other inevitable outcome of failing to negotiate is that it starts out as a molehill but quickly becomes a mountain. The mountain is built foot-by-foot with negative feelings, resentment, and feelings of disempowerment. It is critical to stand up. When you do you will find that others will learn from your example.

I have spoken with a multitude of human resource directors over the years. Each of them has told me the same thing. Their job is to negotiate the best deal they can for the organization. They are tasked with recruiting the best candidates and then getting them in the door at the lowest possible cost. They also shared that the first offer is never the entire budget they have set aside for the new position. They are simply waiting for the candidate to counter with what they believe they should receive. More often than not, candidates become flustered when the offer is presented, and quickly accept it at face value. I have often had clients express concern that if they counter, somehow the original offer will be rescinded. That will not happen. To quote one of the HR professionals with whom I have worked, "I am always astonished when I make an offer and a candidate immediately accepts it. That is because I am sitting there with more money and benefits on the table just waiting for them to ask for it. The majority of candidates never do."

As crass as it may sound, I have often advised clients to stop being so grateful for the original offer. Never, ever accept it. Always be gracious in your response and ask for a day or so to consider it. Then get to work. Research the upper and lower boundaries of the salary for similar roles. Consider where the role is located, and the cost of living associated with that area.

The next issue to consider is what else do you want. Negotiating salary is only part of the process. Do you need help with relocation expenses? What benefits are critical? Do you need a flexible schedule? Career support? Many top executives routinely negotiate for a coach to be retained as they make their way into their new roles. You also want to consider what title most effectively signals to the world what you are going to be doing. Ask for that title. Do not fall into the trap of being told that titles do not matter. They most certainly do.

Everything is negotiable. Almost. There are many shades of gray. This ties back to the work you must do to identify your moral compass and your line in the sand. Remember to keep your non-negotiables in mind when deciding what parameters must be present as you step into a new role. A good rule of thumb is to take the stance that you determine your worth; not a prospective company. Let me reiterate that: you determine your worth. As you travel down your pathway, different seasons of life will find you valuing different things. I watched as a client took a pay cut to travel back to the part of the country where her family lived. She explained to me that at that point in her life she wanted to be close to those she loved more than she wanted to earn a larger paycheck.

In a sense, we have to filter the messages sent to us not only through our development but by society at large. Besides the gender inequality, there are marked discrepancies in opportunity and advancement for minorities. The LGBTQ community faces challenges that others do not. We must, individually and collectively, stand in support of one another and help each other negotiate the best possible scenario for each of us.

I have often heard the sentiment that being liked is very different than being respected. I disagree. You can be very successful at being a strong advocate for yourself in a respectful way. Treat yourself well. Treat others well. Remember that society's messages impact all of us. We must learn to chart our own course without infringing on the rights of others.

At the time of this writing, the extraordinary events that surround the murder of George Floyd are unfolding. It is something that has touched every corner of the world. The tragic message speaks to the heart of what I am trying to convey. Each of us can negotiate our way to success if we are allowed to do so. The emotional theme? "Get your knee off of my neck!" Until we make the playing field level for all of us, we will never be the best version of ourselves.

Part of the message is the fact that you will encounter unfairness. You will find adversarial conditions. Keep going. Keep pushing. I have come to believe that the times that are most uncomfortable are the times that grow and develop you if you use that time to grow and develop. You must be tough. You also can balance that with being gracious and likeable.

One of the key ingredients for success in negotiating is understanding your bottom line. When do you walk away? It is incredibly scary to consider that if you do not understand your moral compass. The other piece that is critical is understanding your finances. If you are not a numbers person, find someone who is and retain them. You have to know where you stand, morally, emotionally, and financially in order to make informed decisions.

Do not confuse negotiation with conflict. It might feel the same at the core of it, but it is not. Negotiating should come from a position of strength that is informed by a thorough sense of self and what is important to you. So many of us run from feelings that seem like conflict because they make us uncomfortable. Do not do that. One strategy is to know where to go for help. Who are your supporters? Activate your squad. Find professionals like financial planners and coaches to help you along the way. And no matter what, never, ever accept the first offer.

Qualities to hone to help you along the way include self-awareness. Intuition is another big one. Remember when we were taught to trust the, "Uh-oh" feeling in our stomach. It is still there. Trust it. Do not become infatuated with an offer to the point that you do not see pitfalls. There is no such thing as a perfect position. It simply does not exist. The idea is to mitigate the pitfalls as much as possible, preferably negotiating about them on the way in the door.

Relational prowess is another quality that will serve you well. Not a people-person? Join a group like Toastmasters to get some experience communicating. Connecting on a human level is so important. Being able to read body language and quickly understand the unwritten rules in a new organization is critical to assimilating.

Resiliency is a quality we all need to cultivate. Although negotiating is a fairly straight-forward and simple process, it is not easy. To clarify, you definitely will encounter times when you will fail at this process. The important thing is to not let those failures keep you down. Get back up. To quote the great philosopher, Rocky Balboa, "Take one step at a time, one punch at a time, one round at a time."

You will surprise yourself. You are stronger than you think. Practicing the art of negotiating will build your confidence. The only way to make a misstep in this area is to fail to take a step at all.

## Chapter 9

# HELPING OTHERS ALONG

*"If you want to lift yourself up, lift up someone else."*
—*Booker T. Washington*

Wherever you find yourself in your journey, you have the ability to help others along. Hear me when I say that every one of us has invaluable lessons to teach others if only we are vulnerable enough to share.

One of the common reasons I hear given when there is a job loss is an explanation that it is politics at play. That may be correct. It can be that you find yourself in a culture that is deeply dysfunctional and there is no way to be successful. Often, it is riddled with something darker and more sinister. Many times, it is because instead of being brought along by others, you may find yourself the target of efforts to ensure that you fail.

Fear drives those efforts. I have talked with people who believe that, in order to be successful, they must hold others down. Somewhere along the way, they have become morally bankrupt to the point that they are willing to harm someone else in order to advance themselves in the short term.

Life has a funny way of righting the ship. Some call it karma. Others call it fate. It may take a long time, but eventually things do come full circle. I want to encourage every person I interact with to spend their time and invest their energy in promoting positivity. Refuse to pull others down. There is enough for all of us. You simply do not have to tear others down to move forward.

I often hear the phrase that we need to put the human back into human resources. I believe that, but I truly believe we need to be sure that we demonstrate humanity. How better to do that than to reach out to one another and help each other along?

It is also true that we find ourselves at different levels of ability to cope with life events, depending on where we are in the journey. A personal crisis can throw us off course, and our need for support may be acute. A unifying event, such as COVID-19 and the resulting pandemic, found everyone affected in an adverse fashion literally at the same time. It is so important to look around and see where you might contribute to the well-being of another.

There is a familiar mantra, "We are all in this together!" Or, "We are all facing the same storm!" These statements may be true, but there is a confounding factor.

We all have a slightly different boat to weather the storm. Be sure to add what you can, when you can, to another's efforts to navigate their boat through the storm. It is not unlike filling up an invisible jar with your efforts. The positive energy that will return to you will see you through a time of need. Make sure you deposit what is necessary, so you do not find yourself holding a jar that is empty.

Earlier I shared about an exchange I had with a division in a university where I made the decision to share that I had been up all night, dealing with a crisis at home that involved a family member who was in the throes of an acute mental health and addiction crisis. That family member was my son. Sharing that openly led to those who approached me later to share that they were also dealing with similar, difficult issues in their families. One other beautiful gift came from that exchange at the end of the day.

A young man approached me who I had come to like a great deal during my time there. He is tall and the picture of health. He is funny, smart, and kind. He is very well liked in his department and throughout the division as a whole.

Joe stood before me and said, "You have given me a great deal to think about today." I responded that I hoped my personal story was not distracting or had somehow lessened the work of the day for him. He did not speak up immediately. I physically watched him make the mental leap to step out in faith and share with me in a very vulnerable way.

He then said, "I have been thinking about the pain and issues I caused my parents during my time struggling with mental health and addiction issues. It has me a little sad."

As I began to apologize, he interrupted me. He continued by explaining that he had been totally unable to hear anything his parents said during that time in his life. He gently told me that he believed my son might never hear his father or me either. He then went on and shocked me as he continued his story.

"Kimberly, I couldn't hear my parents, but I did eventually hear someone else. They helped me. The person who reached me gave me a worry cross and I have kept it to this day. I have been waiting a lot of years to discover who God would tell me to give it to next."

It was at that point that he opened his hand and in his palm was a beautiful wooden cross that had a small groove in the center. He was rubbing his thumb across the groove, helping him to leave his worries there.

I was stunned when he said, "Kimberly, it would be my honor to give it to you."

I began to get a little emotional as I looked at the man who just a few weeks prior had been a total stranger to me. He began to apologize, worried he had upset me. I remember clearly choking out a response. "Joe, I am not upset. Looking at you I feel hopeful. For the first time in quite a while, I feel hopeful. You made it out. Maybe my son will too."

A favorite Bible verse came to my mind as I stood there rubbing my thumb across my new worry cross. *For I know the plans I have for you declares the LORD, plans to prosper you and not to harm you, plans to give you hope and a future. Jeremiah 29:10.*

Joe pulled me up that day. He did it with humanity and humility. He taught me a great lesson. It reinforced for me that by being open and vulnerable about even the most difficult issues, we make ourselves available to receive help and support.

As you invest your time in bringing others along, know that it is an effort that will yield a thousand-fold. The ripple effects of extending support, empathy, wisdom and guidance to others, creates ripple effects that can never fully be measured. Know this. It is one of the most important things you can do for others. The blessings that will return to you will manifest in ways that you cannot begin to imagine. Ralph Waldo Emerson expressed this sentiment in a beautiful way: "To know that even one life has breathed easier because I have lived. That is to have succeeded."

A very worthy way to give back is to serve as a mentor. The most important aspect to remember when establishing mentorship is to pay attention to the relationship that is established. It is similar to pairing a coach with an employee with one notable difference. Like coaching, mentorship establishes a formal connection between two people. Mentorship, however, transcends the coaching process. Mentorship is a relationship that often is lifelong in duration. It also becomes a psychosocial connection. Mentorship provides emotional support along with the advice that is shared regarding career and life management. When it is working at a premium level, mentorship has an open line of communication that flows in both directions. Both the mentor and the mentee benefit equally.

The other unique opportunity that mentorship offers is the fact that you can give back as a mentor, while also benefitting throughout your lifetime as a mentee. Working with more than one mentor at a time is also something to carefully consider. Given the construct of the mentorship relationship, you can reap rewards from accessing mentors for different parts of your life. Look for diversity in the mentorship process. Having mentors from different generational categories, genders, races, and industries are a good place to start. We have so much to teach, and so much to learn from one another.

A good strategy for helping others along is to really probe to understand the root causes that have gotten someone off course. I believe that people rarely fail. In my experience processes do. Many organizations will respond with predictable reasons why one of their employees failed. They will list things like lack of investments and funding to support employees, or not having enough time to properly onboard, orient, and therefore fail at retaining the employee. It is so important to not just list symptoms when helping others along. Dig. Really dig. Gather the knowledge and facts that will illuminate what happened to the person in order to redirect the pathway forward. Then develop a strategy that can be implemented.

Setting priorities must be part of the strategy. Reverse engineering works well in this instance. Define a major goal for one year from now. Then think backwards. What steps must occur, and when, between that date and this day, must they be taken? Drill down to what is important to the person with whom you are attempting to reach. Eliminate distractions. If tasks are identified to be irrelevant to implementing the strategy, take them out of the equation. Providing support and helping others to stay focused is a major gift you can offer.

As you work through priorities there is an interesting exercise that can help others to see when their strengths can tip over into weaknesses. List out identified strengths and the possible downside to each. Some examples? Being enthusiastic is awesome. When enthusiasm is so high it tips over into intimidation, that becomes a weakness. Being decisive is a major strength. If the decisiveness is extreme and therefore argumentative, that is a problem. Tenacity is wonderful and will help navigate the work at hand. Too much tenacity can render one inflexible which is debilitating when one needs to be able to be nimble and pivot. Persistence is a quality to admire. Too much persistence can be annoying! Optimism is a big thumb's up, but too much of it will turn to insincerity. Being agreeable is admirable, but not at the expense of tipping over to avoid confrontation. Directness is usually appreciated, rudeness is not. Humbleness is something to be cultivated. Humbleness that feels manipulative is a weakness. Finally, being results-oriented is a skill that is great in any profession. Results-oriented behavior that causes one to have tunnel vision is a liability in every circumstance.

When you have a thorough list, it will inform your plan of action. Establish goals and then work out a personal development plan to ensure progress. Monitoring progress is key. Prioritize each day's activities. Make certain the priorities are rank ordered in importance. Next, assign the time that should be needed to accomplish each. This will get you into a rhythm that will make certain the goals that were identified for the next year are realized.

According to Tim Stevenson, "You must be thinking ahead in order to lead, and you must be able to articulate your vision and goals."

As you reach out to help others along, remember you are in a unique position of authority. Oftentimes people who need help are already in a fragile state. It is of utmost importance that you weigh your words carefully. You want to be a support, and encourager. Your words weigh more heavily than you might imagine. You may think you are making suggestions, but the person you are helping may hear an order. Criticism must be constructive, honest, and carefully delivered. The power you have to direct the person you are helping is immense. Be responsible with that power. The goal is always to lift one another up.

Incorporating deliberate pursuit of a healthy lifestyle, as well as prioritizing happiness, should be a major part of the strategy. Helping others along to understand where they are in the journey is so important. Empowering people to realize that they have control over their journey, even in the bleakest of circumstances, is powerful. It is equivalent to giving a key to them that allows them to unlock a closed door.

A probing question that will get at real hopes and dreams is, "If I could do anything, I would…"

Use the metaphor of an empty canvas. Place an imaginary paintbrush into the hand of the person you are helping along. Ask them what that picture would look like if they could paint the life they want. Help them to dream. Do not allow them to place a ceiling on their dreams. When you have done the work necessary to build the trust with them, it is amazing what you will be able to help them accomplish.

As the picture comes together, encourage them to paint a picture where they manage their whole life. Encourage transparency. What you should be encouraging is removing barriers to get to the next place. Promoting a healthy work/life balance is a key piece of being successful in these endeavors.

Another responsibility in helping others along is knowing when to push. This should be intuitive if the relationship is strong. All of us experience valleys in our lives. The problem is not the valley. The problem is when someone sets up camp there. It is imperative that time is set aside for grieving losses and dealing with trauma. There has to be an endpoint established. Otherwise, the temptation to remain in the shadows can become very overwhelming. Momentum will be lost, and in the worst-case scenario any progress made will be negated.

To restate a point made often throughout this writing, the power of the human spirit is amazing. Too often people only skim the surface of their true power. When personal changes occur and someone is thrown a curveball, they must be supported and encouraged to focus, and embrace their excellence. Exceptional changes can feel very isolating. Pendulum swings that trigger sudden, extreme change can be terrifying. Helping others who are in this season of their journey is some of the most important work one can do. Those who choose to do it are among God's special people. The most wonderful part is that it is not only one person who benefits as a result. All of us collectively are better when all of us, collectively succeed.

Make time in your life each day to allow the universe to show you ways to give back and help others along. You will find those opportunities if you look around. Integrate it into your life. Your whole life, not just your professional one.

I recently was a recipient of someone helping me along in an area of my life that had nothing at all to do with my work. I had delayed having a knee replacement until I just could not delay it any longer. The day of the surgery found me nervous and second-guessing my decision after all.

As I was transferred to the operating table, the normal activities were happening around me. The medical staff was preparing the room. Several of them were talking to me, asking if I was as comfortable as possible, and if I needed anything. I felt myself overcome with emotion, quite suddenly. For a few seconds I thought about announcing that I had changed my mind. I felt not only emotional, but a little silly. I am a medical professional and knew the chance of anything adverse happening to me was very small. I glanced to the right side of the room and my eyes locked with a woman who was a total stranger to me. She was preparing a surgical tray but had stopped and was watching me quite intently. I know I did not display any signs of overt stress because the others in the room had not noticed the inner dialogue I was having with myself.

This woman had tuned in to what I was experiencing. I could only see her eyes behind her safety goggles. Her hair and the rest of her face was totally covered. Without exchanging one word, she walked towards me. When she was at my side she asked, "Are you doing OK?" I felt my eyes welling with tears and I shook my head slightly. No. I was not doing OK.

She then asked me if I still wanted to have the procedure. I told her I did, and I was not sure why I was having the reaction that had taken over me.

What she did next was wonderful. As a medical professional, I know well what it means to break your sterile field. If you do, you must go through the entire process to scrub your hands and change your gown and gloves. Nevertheless, it is exactly what she did.

She took off her gloves and took my hand in hers. She told me she would stay with me. As I was given the initial medicine that caused me to fall asleep, I had one last memory. That was her hand, tightly grasping mine. It helped me along.

Later, I was never able to discover who the woman was so I could properly thank her. I may not know her name, but I do know this. She stepped up to do something she did not have to do. She put aside what would be the easiest thing for her and placed my needs first. She went the extra step, and because of it, I was able to be successful that morning.

I believe this story closes an important circle. Your first obligation is to yourself. Do the work of self-discovery so you know not only who you are, but what your triggers are, both positive and negative. Work diligently to reinforce the positive and eliminate the negative.

Identify your value system. Know where your ethical line in the sand falls. Protect it.

Take the reins of your life and steer your own course. When traumatic events happen to you, such as the loss of a job, stand in your truth. Search for the blessings that are forthcoming. I promise they are there. Make space in your life to discover what they are.

Once you hit the reset button, celebrate! Know that you will be stronger for having weathered the storm. When the sun rises again, take a good look around. It is uncanny how you can recognize the same signs of stress in others who are experiencing what you have come through. When you see someone sending up a loud, or silent, SOS respond. Share your knowledge and your humanity with the next person in line. Then, step back and observe the ripple effects when that person stops going underwater, breaks the surface and begins to swim towards the shoreline.

Once they are on their way, your final lesson to teach them is to reach back to the next one in line. That way, the circle never ends.

## LESSONS LEARNED

You are you. You are not your job.

Resiliency is key.

Always extend grace.

All of us, every single one, will experience valleys.

You are stronger than you realize.

Your value is intrinsic.

The universe needs your voice.

We all have so much to teach, and so much to learn.

Dream as big as you can, then dream bigger.

Use your paintbrush to paint the canvas of your life.

Surround yourself with people who will pull you up.

It is OK to set boundaries.

You teach people how to treat you.

It is always right to do the right thing.

Practice vulnerability.

There is no substitute for self-empowerment.

Don't set up camp in the valley.

Fall down seven times, get up eight.

Do not ignore your trauma.

Search for opportunities to lift others up.

Ask for help when you need it.

Practice forgiveness purposefully.

You get to write the ending to your story.

YOU ARE THE ARCHITECT OF YOUR LIFE.

Made in the USA
Middletown, DE
28 August 2021